A Brief Exposition
of the Constitution
of the United States

John S. Hart

Solid Ground Christian Books
Birmingham, Alabama USA

OTHER AMERICAN HERITAGE TITLES

In addition to *A Brief Exposition of the Constitution of the United States* by John S. Hart, Solid Ground Christian Books is honored to have the following titles available

Our Lives, Our Fortunes and Our Sacred Honor: *The Lives of the Signers to the Declaration of Independence*
by Charles A. Goodrich

Let the Cannon Blaze Away: *Lectures on the Centennial of American Independence*
by Joseph P. Thompson

The Forgotten Heroes of Liberty: *The Chaplains and Clergy of the American Revolution*
by Joel T. Headley

From the Flag to the Cross: *Scenes and Incidents of Christianity in the Civil War*
by Amos S. Billingsley

A Theological Interpretation of American History by C. Gregg Singer

Visit us at **www.solid-ground-books.com**

A

BRIEF EXPOSITION

OF THE

CONSTITUTION

OF

THE UNITED STATES

FOR THE USE OF

COMMON SCHOOLS.

BY JOHN S. HART, LL.D.,

PRINCIPAL OF THE PHILADELPHIA HIGH SCHOOL, AND PROFESSOR OF MORAL,
MENTAL, AND POLITICAL SCIENCE IN THE SAME; AUTHOR OF AN
ENGLISH GRAMMAR, CLASS BOOK OF POETRY, CLASS
BOOK OF PROSE, ETC., ETC.

PHILADELPHIA:
PUBLISHED BY E. H. BUTLER & CO.
1871.

{ Chamber of the Controllers of Public Schools,
First School District of Pennsylvania.

PHILADELPHIA, *December* 12, 1849.

At a meeting of the Controllers of Public Schools, First District of Penn
sylvania, held at the Controllers' Chamber, on Tuesday, December 11
1849, the following Resolution was adopted :—

Resolved, That Hart's Constitution of the United States be introduced
as a Class Book, into the Grammar Schools of the District.

R. J. HEMPHILL, *Secretary.*

DEPARTMENT OF PUBLIC INSTRUCTION,
Baltimore, Md., July 22d, 1865.

At a meeting of the State Board of Education, held this day, "HART'S CONSTITUTION
OF THE UNITED STATES" was adopted as a Text-Book to be used in the Public Schools
throughout the State.

W. HORACE SOPER,
Clerk.

Solid Ground Christian Books
PO Box 660132
Vestavia Hills AL 35266
205-443-0311
www.solid-ground-books.com

A Brief Exposition of the Constitution of the United States
by John S. Hart (1810-1877)

Reprinted in February 2010

Taken from 1871 edition by E.H. Butler & Co., Philadelphia

Cover design by Borgo Design
Contact at borgogirl@bellsouth.net

ISBN: 978-159925-147-9

PREFACE.

~~~~~~~~~~

EVERY man in this country who holds office, whether Executive, Judicial or Legislative, whether under the National Government or any of the State Governments, is bound by oath to
support the Constitution of the United States. Every one of the
more than two millions who are now entitled to vote, is called
upon to decide questions of Constitutional law, as really and
truly as is the Supreme Court of the United States. But how
many of all that number have ever read the Constitution? In
what proportion of our Colleges, Academies, or Common Schools
is it studied? In what system of education, whether public or
private, in any part of the country, is a knowledge of the Constitution of the country made a requisite for graduation, or for
admission from a lower school to a higher one? Ask a number
of boys at school almost any reasonable question in Geography or
History, and you will see dozens ready to reply without a
moment's hesitation. But ask them what will be necessary,
when they grow up, to entitle them to vote, what constitutes
citizenship, what rights a citizen of one State has in another
State, or any other simple and obvious question in regard to the
Constitution of their country, and you will be met with a profound silence. And is not a knowledge of his immediate personal rights and duties quite as important to the young American,
as to be acquainted with a long catalogue of dead kings or
distant cities?

The main reason why the study of the Constitution has never
yet been made a branch of Common School education is believed

to be an entire misapprehension in regard to the nature and difficulty of the study. There are, it is true, not a few passages in the Constitution, the proper construction of which has given rise to much discussion; and there are many nice points arising out of its more obvious provisions, requiring for their solution great natural abilities and profound legal erudition. But it is still true, that the great majority of its clauses are as intelligible, and as easily remembered as most of the studies which now make an essential part in every system of education. What difficu.ty is there in a boy's learning that a Representative is chosen for two years, while a Senator is chosen for six, that a Representative must be twenty-five years old, while a Senator must be thirty, to know what body has the power to impeach, and what the power to try impeachments, in short to understand and recollect nine out of ten of all the provisions of the Constitution? Is it one whit more difficult than to comprehend and recollect the various details of Geography and History, to give off-hand the position of Timbuctoo or the Tagus, or to know in what year Rome was founded or Cæsar slain?

The plan pursued in this little book is in accordance with the views here suggested. There has been no attempt to discuss knotty political questions, or to speculate upon abstract theories of government, but simply to present the Constitution itself, with such questions and answers, as might direct the attention of the learner to its plain and obvious meaning. The Constitution provides for the duties and rights of every day life, and is written in simple language almost entirely free from technical and professional expressions. Is there any reason why children capable of learning, and teachers capable of teaching History and Geography, might not intelligently study and teach all its material facts and provisions, as they are here presented?

CONTENTS.

(5)

ARTICLE II. EXECUTIVE DEPARTMENT.

AMENDMENTS TO THE CONSTITUTION.

AMENDMENTS ADDED SINCE 1871

NOTABLE QUOTES ON THE CONSTITUTION

"It is every Americans' right and obligation to read and interpret the Constitution for himself." — Thomas Jefferson

"Hold on, my friends, to the Constitution and to the Republic for which it stands. Miracles do not cluster, and what has happened once in 6000 years, may not happen again. Hold on to the Constitution, for if the American Constitution should fail, there will be anarchy throughout the world." — Daniel Webster

"Every act of a delegated authority, contrary to the tenor of the commission under which it is exercised, is void. No legislative act, therefore, contrary to the Constitution, can be valid. To deny this, would be to affirm, that the deputy is greater than his principal; that the servant is above his master; that the representatives of the people are superior to the people themselves; that men acting by virtue of powers, may do not only what their powers do not authorize, but what they forbid." — Alexander Hamilton

"On every question of construction, let us carry ourselves back to the time when the Constitution was adopted, recollect the spirit manifested in the debates, and instead of trying what meaning may be squeezed out of the text, or invented against it, conform to the probable one in which it was passed."
— Thomas Jefferson

"The particular phraseology of the Constitution of the United States confirms and strengthens the principle, supposed to be essential to all written constitutions, that a law repugnant to the Constitution is void; and that courts, as well as other departments, are bound by that instrument." — John Marshall

More Notable Quotes

"God governs in the affairs of man. And if a sparrow cannot fall to the ground without his notice, is it probable that an empire can rise without His aid? We have been assured in the Sacred Writings that except the Lord build the house, they labor in vain that build it. I firmly believe this. I also believe that, without His concurring aid, we shall succeed in this political building no better than the builders of Babel"
— Benjamin Franklin, Constitutional Convention of 1787, original manuscript of this speech

"That the said Constitution shall never be construed to authorize Congress to infringe the just liberty of the press or the rights of conscience; or to prevent the people of the United States who are peaceable citizens from keeping their own arms..." — Samuel Adams

"Besides the advantage of being armed, which the Americans possess over the people of almost every other nation ... notwithstanding the military establishments in the several kingdoms of Europe, which are carried as far as the public resources will bear, the governments are afraid to trust the people with arms." — James Madison, author of the Bill of Rights, in Federalist Paper No. 46

"It is in vain, Sir, to extenuate the matter. Gentlemen may cry, Peace, Peace! But there is no peace. The war is actually begun! The next gale that sweeps from the North will bring to our ears the clash of resounding arms! Our brethren are already in the field! Why stand we here idle? What is it that Gentlemen want? What would they have? Is life so dear, or peace so sweet, as to be purchased at the price of chains and slavery? Forbid it, Almighty God! I know not what course others may take, but as for me, give me liberty or give me death!" — Patrick Henry, in his famous "The War Inevitable" speech, March, 1775

A

Brief

Exposition

of the

CONSTITUTION

of the

UNITED STATES

CONSTITUTION

OF THE

UNITED STATES.

~~~~~~~~~~

INTRODUCTION.

1. What kind of government existed in the American Colonies prior to the Revolution?

A Colonial Government.

2. What three forms of colonial government were there?

The Provincial, Proprietary, and Charter Governments.

3. What were the Provincial Governments?

The Provincial Governments were those under the immediate control of the King of Great Britain.

4. What were the Proprietary Governments?

The Proprietary Governments were those under the immediate control of Proprietaries, who received grants to that effect in letters patent from the King.

5. What were the Charter Governments?

The Charter Governments were those under the immediate control of the King, but having certain important political rights secured to them by charter.

6. What Colonies, at the time of the Revolution, were under Provincial Governments?

New Hampshire, New York, New Jersey, Virginia, North Carolina, South Carolina, and Georgia.

7. What Colonies were governed by Proprietaries at the commencement of the Revolution?

(13)

Pennsylvania, Delaware, and Maryland.

8. What Colonies were under Charter Governments at the time of the Revolution ?

Massachusetts, Connecticut, and Rhode Island.

9. When was a general convention of delegates from the severa. Colonies first called ?

In September, 1774.

10. What was this Convention called ?

The Continental Congress.

11. What important state paper did the first Continental Congress prepare ?

The Bill of Rights.

12. When did the next Congress assemble ?

In May, 1775.

13. What decisive step did they take ?

They declared the united colonies independent.

14. When was the Declaration of Independence adopted ?

On the 4th of July, 1776.

15. What powers were assumed by the Continental Congress ?

They assumed all the powers of sovereignty necessary to maintain the safety and independence of the united colonies.

16. What was the character of these powers ?

They were revolutionary.

17. How is the exercise of these powers by the Continental Congress justified from the charge of usurpation ?

The exercise of these powers was required by the necessity of the case, and was acquiesced in by the people.

18. How long did the Continental Congress continue to be the National Government ?

Until March, 1781, near the close of the Revolutionary War.

19 What frame of government was then adopted ?

The Articles of Confederation.

20. What was the great defect in the Articles of Confederation?

The want of sufficient power in the General Govern ment.

21. When did the present Constitution go into operation?

In September, 1788.

22. What is the introductory paragraph of the Constitution called?

The Preamble.

THE PREAMBLE.

"*We, the People of the United States, in order to form a more perfect union, establish justice, insure domestic tranquillity, provide for the common defence, promote the general welfare, and secure the blessings of liberty to ourselves and our posterity, do ordain and establish this Constitution for the United States of America.*"

23. What is the main object of the Preamble?

The main object of the Preamble is to set forth the purposes for which the Constitution was adopted.

24. What were the purposes for which the Constitution was ordained and established?

1st, To form a more perfect union; 2d, To establish justice; 3d, To insure domestic tranquillity; 4th, To provide for the common defence; 5th, To promote the general welfare; and 6th, To secure the blessings of liberty to ourselves and our posterity.

25. Why is this part of the Preamble important?

Because the purposes for which the Constitution was adopted form a valuable aid in interpreting its principles.

26. What else is contained in the Preamble?

It sets forth the parties who established the Constitution.

27. Who are declared in the Preamble to have established the Constitution?

The people of the United States.

28. How does the Constitution compare in this respect with the articles of Confederation ?

The Articles of Confederation emanated from *the States;* the Constitution of the United States emanated directly from *the People.*

29. Why is this part of the Preamble important ?

Because it shows the authority upon which the Constitution rests.

GENERAL PRINCIPLES.

30. Into how many departments is the government of the United States divided ?

Into three ; — *Legislative, Executive,* and *Judicial.*

31. What is the *Legislative power ?*

The power which makes the laws.

32. What is the *Executive power ?*

The power which carries the laws into effect.

33. What is the *Judicial power?*

The power which interprets the laws.

34. What may be remarked in regard to this separation of the powers of Government ?

It is indispensable to the existence of good government.

35. What kind of government is that in which these powers are all vested in the same hands ?

It is an absolute government, or despotism.

36. Why is such a government dangerous ?

Because it gives no security against the abuse of power.

37. To what do the three main articles of the Constitution relate ?

To the distribution of the powers of government among the three departments, the Legislative, the Executive, and the Judicial.

38. To what does Article I. relate ?

To the Legislative Department.

ARTICLE I. THE LEGISLATIVE DEPARTMENT.

SECTION I. *Congress in general.*

"All legislative powers herein granted, shall be vested in a Congress of the United States, which shall consist of a Senate and House of Representatives."

39. To what does this section relate ?

To the establishment of the National Legislature.

40. In what body are the legislative powers of the United States vested ?

All Legislative powers granted in this Constitution are vested in a Congress of the United States.

41. Of what does the Congress of the United States consist ?

Of a Senate and House of Representatives.

42. What advantage is there in dividing the legislative body into two branches ?

The two Houses of Congress act as a check upon each other.

43. Repeat Section I.

SECTION II. *House of Representatives.*

CLAUSE I. *"The House of Representatives shall be composed of members chosen every second year by the people of the several States, and the electors in each State shall have the qualifications requisite for electors of the most numerous branch of the State legislature."*

44. To what does this clause refer ?

To the organization of the House of Representatives.

45. How often are the members of the House of Representatives chosen ?

Every second year.

46 Why is a comparatively short term of service fixed for the House of Representatives ?

That they may come more frequently and more directly under the supervision of popular opinion.

47. By whom are they chosen ?

By the People of the several States.

48. What qualifications are requisite to enable a citizen in any State to vote for members of the National House of Representatives ?

The same qualifications which are necessary to enable him to vote for the most numerous branch of the State legislature.

49. Repeat the words of Clause I.

CLAUSE II. "*No person shall be a Representative, who shall not have attained the age of twenty-five years, and been seven years a citizen of the United States, and who shall not, when elected, be an inhabitant of that State in which he shall be chosen.*"

50. To what does this clause relate?

To the qualifications of the Representatives.

51. How old must a Representative be ?

No person shall be a Representative, who shall not have attained the age of twenty-five years.

52. How long must he have been a citizen of the United States ?

Seven years.

53. What is necessary in regard to residence ?

He must, when elected, be an inhabitant of that State in which he is chosen.

54. Repeat the words of Clause II.

CLAUSE III. " *Representatives and direct taxes shall be apportioned among the several States which may be inclu-*

ded *within this Union, according to their respective num-bers, which shall be determined by adding to the whole number of free persons, including those bound to service for a term of years, and excluding Indians not taxed, three-fifths of all other persons. The actual enumeration shall be made within three years after the first meeting of the Congress of the United States, and within every subsequent term of ten years, in such manner as they shall by law di-rect. The number of Representatives shall not exceed one for every thirty thousand, but each State shall have at least one Representative; and until such enumeration shall be made, the State of New Hampshire shall be entitled to choose three, Massachusetts eight, Rhode Island and Pro-vidence Plantations one, Connecticut five, New York six, New Jersey four, Pennsylvania eight, Delaware one, Ma-ryland six, Virginia ten, North Carolina five, South Ca-rolina five, and Georgia three.*

55. To what does this clause relate?

To the Apportionment of Representatives and direct taxes among the States.

56. In what manner are Representatives and direct taxes appor tioned among the several States?

According to their respective numbers.

57. In determining the number to be represented in the different States, are any counted besides free persons?

Yes.

58. Who are meant by "those bound to service for a term of years?"

Apprentices.

59. What is provided in regard to apprentices?

They are included in the number of free persons.

60. What is provided in regard to Indians?

Indians *not taxed* are to be excluded from the num-ber of free persons.

61. How then is the whole number of free persons to be obtained ?

By including in that number apprentices, and excluding Indians not taxed.

62. When the whole number of free persons is thus ascertained, what must be added in order to determine the number to be represented ?

Three-fifths of all other persons.

63. Who are particularly meant by "other persons ?"

Slaves. N. B. This part of the clause has been repealed by the adoption of the Fourteenth Amendment.

64. Repeat that part of the 3d clause which relates to the mode of apportioning the Representatives among the States, after the enumeration.

" Representatives and direct taxes shall be apportioned among the several States which may be included within this Union, according to their respective numbers, which shall be determined by adding to the whole number of free persons, including those bound to service for a term of years, and excluding Indians not taxed, three-fifths of all other persons."

65. When was the first enumeration to be made ?

Within three years after the first meeting of Congress.

66. When was it actually made ?

In 1790.

67. How often was the census to be taken afterwards ?

Once in every ten years.

68. How was the enumeration to be made ?

In such a manner as Congress should, by law, direct

69. Repeat that part of the Apportionment clause which relates to the time and mode of making the enumeration.

" The actual enumeration shall be made within three years after the first meeting of the Congress of the United States, and within every subsequent term of ten years, in such manner as they shall by law direct."

70. Repeat that part of the Apportionment clause which limits the number of Representatives.

" The number of Representatives shall not exceed one for every thirty thousand, but each State shall have at least one Representative."

71. How many Representatives was each of the States entitled to choose until the first enumeration should be made?

" The State of New Hampshire was entitled to choose 3

"	"	Massachusetts	-	-	-	8
"	"	Rhode Island and Providence Plantations				1
"	"	Connecticut	-	-	-	5
"	"	New York	-	-	-	6
"	"	New Jersey	-	-	-	4
"	"	Pennsylvania	-	-	-	8
"	"	Delaware	-	-	-	1
"	"	Maryland	-	-	-	6
"	"	Virginia	-	-	-	10
"	"	North Carolina		-	-	5
"	"	South Carolina		-	-	5
"	"	Georgia	-	-	-	3

Total, *65

72. When was the last apportionment made?
In 1861.

73. By what census is that apportionment determined?
By the census of 1860.

74. What is the ratio of representation under that apportionment?
One Representative for every 126,932, and an additional member is allowed to each State in which the remaining fraction exceeds one-half of that number.

75. What is the whole number of Representatives under this apportionment in 1867 ?
Two hundred and forty-three.

---

* The original apportionment is given for reference merely, because it is included in the body of the Constitution. The present apportionment (p. 22), however, should be learned instead of the original one.

				Admitted into the Union
1.	New York has	31	representatives.	1776
2.	Pennsylvania	24	"	1776
3.	Virginia	8	"	1776
4.	Massachusetts	10	"	1776
5.	Georgia	7	"	1776
6.	North Carolina	7	"	1776
7.	Maryland	5	"	1776
8.	New Jersey	5	"	1776
9.	Connecticut	4	"	1776
10.	South Carolina	4	"	1776
11.	New Hampshire	3	"	1776
12.	Delaware	1	"	1776
13.	Rhode Island	2	"	1776
14.	Vermont	3	"	1791
15.	Kentucky	9	"	1792
16.	Tennessee	8	"	1796
17.	Ohio	19	"	1802
18.	Louisiana	5	"	1812
19.	Indiana	11	"	1816
20.	Mississippi	5	"	1817
21.	Illinois	14	"	1818
22.	Alabama	6	"	1819
23.	Maine	5	"	1820
24.	Missouri	9	"	1821
25.	Arkansas	3	"	1836
26.	Michigan	6	"	1837
27.	Florida	1	"	1845
28.	Iowa	6	"	1845
29.	Texas	4	"	1845
30.	Wisconsin	6	"	1848
31.	California	3	"	1850
32.	Minnesota	2	"	1858
33.	Oregon	1	"	1859
34.	Kansas	1	"	1860
35.	West-Virginia	3	"	1862
36.	Nevada	1	"	1864
37.	Nebraska	1	"	1867

243

CLAUSE IV.—"*When vacancies happen in the represen-*
tation from any State, the executive authority thereof shall
issue writs of election to fill such vacancies."

78. To what does this clause relate?

To filling vacancies in the House of Representatives.

79. How are the vacancies in the Representation from any State
to be filled?

The Executive of that State shall issue writs of
election to fill such vacancies.

80. Repeat the words of Clause IV.

CLAUSE V.—"*The House of Representatives shall*
choose their Speaker and other officers; and shall have
the sole power of impeachment."

81. How are the Speaker and other officers of the House appointed?

By the House itself.

82. Why is it important that the Speaker and other officers should
be chosen by the House?

It gives the House a more efficient control over
its officers.

83. What is the power of impeachment?

It is the right which the Representatives have to
bring an accusation against high officers of government, for maladministration of office.

84. Are impeachments tried by the House?

They are not; they are tried by the Senate.

85. Repeat Clause V.

———

SECTION III. *Senate.*

CLAUSE I. "*The Senate of the United States shall be*
composed of two Senators from each State, chosen by the
Legislature thereof, for six years; and each Senator shall
have one vote."

86. To what does this clause relate?

To the organization of the Senate.

87. What advantage is to be derived from dividing the legislative body into two branches?

The two Houses act as a check upon each other.

88. How is this check most effectually secured?

By making the two Houses dissimilar in their organization.

89. In what respects is the organization of the Senate different from that of the House of Representatives?

The Senate differs from the House of Representatives in regard to the number of members, the mode of election, and the term of service.

90. Of how many members is the Senate composed?

Of two from each State, or sixty-eight in all.

91. How are the Senators chosen?

By the Legislatures of the several States.

92. How do they differ in this respect from the Representatives?

The Representatives are chosen by the people of the States.

93. For what time are the Senators chosen?

For six years.

94. How do they differ in this respect from the Representatives?

The Representatives are chosen for only two years.

95. Why is a comparatively long term of service fixed for the Senators?

That they may serve as a check upon the sudden fluctuations of popular opinion, to which the other branch of the Legislature is liable.

96. In what manner do the Senators vote?

Each Senator has one vote.

97. How did the Continental Congress vote?

By States; the Representatives from each State having but one vote.

98. Repeat Clause I

CLAUSE II. " *Immediately after they shall be assembled* *in consequence of the first election, they shall be divided,* *as equally as may be, into three classes.   The seats of the* *Senators of the first class shall be vacated at the expira* *tion of the second year ; of the second class, at the expi-* *ration of the fourth year; and of the third class, at the ex-* *piration of the sixth year ; so that one-third may be chosen* *every second year; and if vacancies happen by resignation,* *or otherwise, during the recess of the legislature of any* *State, the executive thereof may make temporary appoint-* *ments until the next meeting of the legislature, which shall* *then fill such vacancies.*"

99. To what does the first part of this clause relate ?

To the division of the Senators into classes.

100. Into how many classes were the Senators divided?

Three.

101. How long did the Senators of each class hold their seats?

Those of the first class held their seats for two years, those of the second class for four years, and those of the third class for six years.

102. What proportion of the Senators, in consequence of this arrangement, is chosen every second year ?

One-third.

103. What is the object of this arrangement?

By means of this arrangement, one branch of the Legislature always contains a considerable number of members well versed in the public business.

104. Repeat that part of the clause which relates to the arrangement of the Senators into classes.

" Immediately after they shall be assembled, in consequence of the first election, they shall be divided, as equally as may be, into three classes.   The seats of the Senators of the first class shall be vacated at the expiration of the second year ; of the second class, at the expiration of the fourth year; and of tne third class, at the expiration of the sixth year; so that one-third may be chosen every second year."

105. To what does the latter part of the clause relate?

To filling vacancies.

106. How are vacancies in the Senate filled?

By the appointment of the Legislature of the State in whose representation the vacancy may exist.

107. If the vacancies happen during the recess of the legislature of the State, how shall they be filled?

The Executive of the State may make temporary appointments until the next meeting of the Legislature.

108. Repeat that part of the clause which relates to *vacancies.*

" If vacancies happen by resignation, or otherwise, during the recess of the Legislature of any State, the Executive thereof may make temporary appointments until the next meeting of the Legislature, which shall then fill such vacancies."

CLAUSE III. *" No person shall be a Senator whu shall not have attained to the age of thirty years, and been nine years a citizen of the United States, and who shall not, when elected, be an inhabitant of that State for which he shall be chosen."*

109. To what does this clause relate?

To the qualifications of the Senators.

110. How old must a Senator be?

At least thirty years.

111. How long must he have been a citizen of the United States?

At least nine years.

112. What is required in regard to residence?

He must, at the time of his election, be an inhabitant of that State for which he shall be chosen.

113. In what respects do the qualifications of a Senator differ from those of a Representative?

A Senator must be thirty years old, and have been a citizen nine years; a Representative need be only twenty-five years old, and have been a citizen only seven years.

114. Repeat Clause III.

CLAUSE IV. " *The Vice-President of the United States shall be President of the Senate, but shall have no vote, unless they be equally divided.*"

115. To what does this clause relate?

To the Presiding Officer of the Senate.

116. Who is constituted President of the Senate?

The Vice-President of the United States.

117. When is he entitled to vote?

Only when the Senate is equally divided.

118. Why was not the Senate allowed to choose a presiding officer from its own members?

For fear of giving too much influence to that State whose Senator should be selected to preside.

119. Why is there not the same danger in the House of Representatives?

Because the House of Representatives is so much more numerous.

120. Repeat Clause IV.

CLAUSE V. " *The Senate shall choose their other officers, and also a President* pro tempore, *in the absence of the Vice-President, or when he shall exercise the office of President of the United States.*

121. To what does this clause relate?

To the appointment of the other officers of the Senate.

122. How are these officers chosen?

By the Senate itself.

123 When do they choose a President *pro tempore?*

When the President of the Senate is absent, or exercises the office of President of the United States.

124. Repeat Clause V.

CLAUSE VI. " *The Senate shall have the sole power to try all impeachments. When sitting for that purpose, they shall be on oath or affirmation. When the President of the United States is tried, the Chief Justice shall preside; and no person shall be convicted without the concurrence of two-thirds of the members present.*"

125. To what does Clause VI. relate?

The trial of impeachments.

126. By whom are impeachments to be tried?

By the Senate only.

127. Why could not impeachments be tried by the Supreme Court?

Because the questions involved are of a political rather than of a legal character.

128. In what respect does the Senate, when sitting for the trial of impeachments, deviate from its usual mode of proceeding.

When sitting for the trial of impeachments, the Senate shall be on oath or affirmation.

129. What is the object of this provision?

To give greater solemnity to the proceedings.

130. Who shall preside in the Senate on the trial of the President of the United States?

The Chief Justice.

131. What is necessary in order to convict a person on impeachment?

The concurrence of two-thirds of the members present.

132. Why should not the verdict be unanimous, as in a trial by jury?

In consequence of the influence of political feelings, few persons could ever be convicted.

133. Why should not a bare majority be sufficient to convict?

In consequence of the influence of political feelings, few persons would ever be safe from conviction.

134. Repeat Clause VI.

CLAUSE VII. *"Judgment in cases of impeachment shall not extend further than to removal from office, and disqualification to hold and enjoy any office of honour, trust, or profit, under the United States; but the party convicted shall, nevertheless, be liable and subject to indictment, trial, judgment, and punishment, according to law."*

135. To what does this Clause relate?

To the judgment to be rendered in cases of impeachment.

136. How is the judgment, in cases of impeachment, limited?

It shall not extend further than to removal from office, and disqualification to hold office under the United States.

137. Are those convicted on impeachment liable to suffer no other punishment?

They are afterwards liable to indictment, trial, judgment and punishment, according to law, before the ordinary courts of justice.

138. Repeat Clause VII.

SECTION IV. *Both Houses.*

CLAUSE I. *" The times, places, and manner, of holding elections for Senators and Representatives, shall be prescribed in each State by the Legislature thereof: but the Congress may at any time, by law, make or alter such regulations, except as to the places of choosing Senators."*

139. To what does this clause relate?

The election of Members of Congress.

140. In whom is the power of regulating their election vested?

In the Legislature of each State.

141. In what particulars may the Legislature of each State regu late the election of Members of Congress?

They may prescribe the times, places, and manner of holding the election.

142. Why should these particulars be determined in the several States by their own Legislatures?

Because the people of the several States can judge best in regard to their own local conveniences.

143. What power has Congress in the matter?

Congress may by law, make or alter such regula tions, except as to the place of choosing Senators.

144. Why is the power of making or altering these regulations given to Congress?

Because the State Legislatures might neglect to provide duly for such elections, or might make such provisions as would embarrass the operation of the General Government.

145. Why is not the *place of choosing Senators* also left to the discretion of Congress?

Because the Senators are elected by the State Le-gislatures, whose place of meeting is left to be decided by their own convenience, with respect to their ordi-nary duties.

146. Repeat Clause I.

CLAUSE II. " *The Congress shall assemble at least once in every year, and such meeting shall be on the first Mon-day in December, unless they shall by law appoint a dif-ferent day.*"

147. To what does this clause refer?

To the assembling of Congress.

148. How often shall Congress assemble?

The Congress shall assemble at least once in **every** year.

149. What day is fixed for the meeting of Congress?

The first Monday of December, unless they, by law, appoint a different day.

150. What would have been the consequence of omitting to make in the Constitution any provision in regard to the meeting of Congress?

The time of assembling would have been left to the determination of Congress itself, or of some other department of the government.

151. What danger would there have been in this?

In times of corruption, or usurpation, Government might omit or postpone the meeting of Congress, for the purpose of preventing a redress of grievances.

152. Repeat Clause II.

———

Section V. *The Houses separately.*

Clause I. " *Each House shall be the judge of the elections, returns, and qualifications, of its own members, and a majority of each shall constitute a quorum to do business; but a smaller number may adjourn from day to day, and may be authorized to compel the attendance of absent members, in such manner, and under such penalties, as each House may provide.*"

153. To what does the first part of this clause relate?

To the mode of ascertaining the right of any one o a seat in Congress.

154. Who are to judge of the right of any one to a seat in either House?

Each House is the judge of the elections, returns and qualifications of its own members.

155. Why should each House have the exclusive right to judge of the qualifications of its members?

Because in no other way could it maintain the ne cessary degree of independence.

156. To what does the next item in this clause relate?

To a quorum.

157. What is a quorum?

The number of any assembly necessary to transact business.

158. Why is it necessary to forbid the transaction of business unless there is a certain number of the members present?

To prevent laws being passed by stealth, when, by some accident, only a small portion of the legislators are present.

159. What number of each House of Congress is necessary to constitute a quorum?

A majority.

160. What powers have a smaller number than the majority?

They may adjourn from day to day, and may be authorized to compel the attendance of absent members, in such manner and under such penalties as each House may provide.

161. Why is this power given to the minority of a Legislative Assembly?

Otherwise it would be in the power of a portion of the members, by voluntarily absenting themselves, to suspend legislation.

162. Repeat Clause I.

CLAUSE II. " *Each House may determine the rules of its proceedings, punish its members for disorderly beha- viour, and, with the concurrence of two-thirds, expel a member.*"

163. To what does this clause relate?

To the maintenance of order.

164. Who determines the rules of proceeding in Congress?

Each House may determine its own rules of proceeding.

165. What means has each House for enforcing its rules?

Each House has the power to punish its own members for disorderly behaviour; and, with the consent of two-thirds, to expel a member.

CLAUSE III. " *Each House shall keep a journal of its proceedings, and, from time to time, publish the same, excepting such parts as may, in their judgment, require secrecy ; and the yeas and nays of the members of either House, on any question, shall, at the desire of one-fifth of those present, be entered on the journal.*"

166. What is the object of the first part of this clause?

To ensure publicity to all the Acts of Congress.

167. How is the publicity of the proceedings in Congress secured?

By compelling each House to keep a journal of its proceedings, and to publish the same from time to time.

168. How much of its Journal is each House required to publish?

All except such parts as may, in their judgment, require secrecy.

169. To what does the latter part of the clause relate?

The responsibility of individual members for their votes.

170. How is responsibility of individual members secured?

By requiring the yeas and nays to be taken on any question, at the desire of one-fifth of the members present.

171. What is meant by taking the yeas and nays on any question?

Recording on the journal the names of those who vote on each side, and not merely the number of votes.

172. Repeat Clause III.

CLAUSE IV. *" Neither House, during the session of Con-gress, shall, without the consent of the other, adjourn for more than three days, nor to any other place than that in which the two Houses shall be sitting."*

173. What does this clause contain?

Restrictions upon the power of adjournment.

174. What is the object of these restrictions?

To prevent either House from interrupting the re-gular course of legislation.

175. For how long a time may either House adjourn without the consent of the other?

For three days.

176. How else is each House limited with regard to its own adjournment?

It cannot adjourn to any other place than that in which the two Houses may be sitting.

177. Repeat Clause IV.

———

SECTION VI. *Privileges and Disabilities of Members.*

CLAUSE I. *"The Senators and Representatives shall re-ceive a compensation for their services, to be ascertained by law, and paid out of the Treasury of the United States. They shall, in all cases, except treason, felony, and breach of the peace, be privileged from arrest during their attend-ance at the session of their respective Houses, and in going to, and returning from, the same; and for any speech or debate in either House, they shall not be questioned in any other place.'*

178. To what does the first part of this clause refer?

To the compensation of Members of Congress.

179. What provision is made for this?

Members of Congress shall receive a compensatior for their services, to be ascertained by law, and paid out of the treasury of the United States.

180. What objection has been made to giving a compensation to Members of Congress?

Some have feared it might lead unworthy persons to seek the office for mercenary motives.

181. What reason has been assigned for giving a compensation?

The expenses of the office might deter men of talent and worth from seeking it, and so give an undue advantage to men of wealth.

182. To what does the next part of this clause relate?

Freedom from arrest.

183. How far do Members of Congress enjoy the privilege of freedom from arrest?

During their attendance at the session of their respective Houses, and in going to and returning from the same.

184. What exception is made to this privilege?

Members are not privileged in cases of treason, felony, and breach of the peace.

185. What is the object of exempting a Member of Congress from arrest?

To prevent his constituents from being deprived of their right of Representation.

186. To what does the latter part of this clause refer?

To the freedom of debate.

187. What privilege do Members of Congress enjoy in this respect?

For any speech or debate in either House, they shall not be questioned in any other place.

188 What is the object of this privilege?

To secure the utmost freedom in discussing the public interests.

189. What means are there of preventing members from abusing the privilege of freedom in debate?

For any abuse of this privilege, the members are accountable to the House to which they belong.

190. Repeat Clause I.

CLAUSE II. " *No Senator or Representative shall, during the time for which he was elected, be appointed to any civil office under the authority of the United States, which shall have been created, or the emoluments whereof shall have been increased, during such time; and no person, holding any office under the United States, shall be a member of either House during his continuance in office.*"

191. To what does this clause relate?

To the disabilities of Members of Congress.

192. To what offices are the Senators and Representatives ineligible, during the time for which they were elected to Congress?

They are ineligible to any civil office, under the authority of the United States, which shall have been created, or the emoluments whereof shall have been increased during such time.

193. May Members of Congress be appointed to offices already existing?

They may, provided the emoluments of the same are not increased during the time for which said members were elected.

194. What is the object in excluding Members of Congress from being appointed to new offices, or to those whose emoluments are increased during their term of membership?

That they may not be induced to vote for such offices, or such increase of the emoluments of the same, for the sake of being appointed to them.

195. To what other disability are Members liable?

They cannot at the same time be Members of Con-gress, and hold office under the United States.

196. If a Member of Congress be appointed to any office under the United States, what must he do before he can accept it?

He must first resign his seat in Congress.

197. If any person holding office under the United States, wishes to become a Member of Congress, what must he do?

He must first resign his office.

198. Repeat Clause II.

SECTION VII. *Mode of Passing Laws.*

CLAUSE I. "*All bills for raising revenue shall ori-ginate in the House of Representatives ; but the Senate may propose or concur with amendments, as on other bills.*"

199. To what does this clause relate?
To Revenue Bills.

200. Where must all Bills for raising a revenue originate?
In the House of Representatives.

201. Why is the power of originating Bills for revenue confined to the House of Representatives?

Because they are the more immediate Representa-tives of the people.

202. Has the Senate no power over a revenue bill?

They may propose amendments to it, as to other bills.

203. Repeat Clause I.

CLAUSE II. "*Every bill which shall have passed the House of Representatives and the Senate, shall, before it become a law, be presented to the President of the United States ; if he approve, he shall sign it, but if not, he shall return it, with his objections, to that House in which*" *it shall have originated, who shall enter the objections at large on their journal, and proceed to reconsider it. If, after such reconsideration, two-thirds of that House shall agree to pass the bill, it shall be sent, together with the objections, to the other House, by which it shall likewise be reconsidered, and, if approved by two-thirds of that House, it shall become a law. But in all such cases the votes of both Houses shall be determined by yeas and nays and the names of the persons voting for and against the bill shall be entered on the journal of each House, respectively. If any bill shall not be returned by the President within ten days (Sundays excepted) after it shall have been presented to him, the same shall be a law, in like manner as if he had signed it, unless the Congress, by their adjournment, prevent its return, in which case it shall not be a law."*

204. To what does this clause refer?

To the power of the President over the passage of a bill.

205. After a bill has passed both Houses of Congress, what must be done with it?

It must be presented to the President.

206. What is still necessary before it can become a law?

The President must approve and sign it.

207. What must the President do if he does not approve it?

He must return it, with his objections.

208. To which House must it be returned?

To the House in which it originated.

209. What is this power of the President, of objecting to the passage of a Bill, called?

The Veto power.

210. What is the meaning of the word *veto?*

I forbid.

211 From whom are both the word and the custom derived?

From the Romans, where the Tribunes of the People had the power of forbidding the passage of any law.

212. What is the object of vesting this power in the hands of the President?

It is intended to act as a check upon improper legislation.

213. Why would the President be likely to view a Bill differently from Congress?

Because of the difference in the nature of his office, and in the mode of his appointment.

214. In what important particulars may the Veto power be useful?

In resisting encroachments of the Legislature upon the other departments of Government, and in preventing immature and hasty legislation.

215. When the President has returned a Bill, with his objections to the House in which it originated, what must they do?

They shall enter the objections of the President at large on their journals, and proceed to reconsider it.

216. If, on reconsideration by the House in which it originated, the Bill receives a vote of less than two-thirds, what becomes of it?

It is lost.

217. If it is repassed by a vote of two-thirds of that House, what is next to be done?

They shall send it, together with the President's objections, to the other House.

218. What shall the other House do?

They shall likewise proceed to reconsider it.

219. If they fail to pass it by a vote of two-thirds, what becomes of it?

It is lost.

220. If they also, on reconsideration, pass it by a vote of two thirds, what becomes of it?

It becomes a law, without the signature of the President.

221. Why might not a Bill, which passed originally by a vote of two-thirds of both Houses, become a law at once, without the signature of the President?

Because members might change their opinions after receiving the objections of the President.

222. How shall the votes of the two Houses on a Bill which has been vetoed, be determined?

By yeas and nays; the names of the persons voting for and against the bill being entered on the journal of each House respectively.

223. In what other way may a Bill become a law without the signature of the President?

If the President neglects or refuses to return it within ten days (Sundays excepted,) after it shall have been presented to him, the same shall be a law in like manner as if he had signed it.

224. What exception is made to this provision?

If Congress, by their adjournment before the expiration of the ten days, prevent its return, it shall not become a law. .

225. Repeat that portion of the second clause which relates to the approval or veto of a Bill.

" Every bill, which shall have passed the House of Representatives and the Senate, shall, before it become a law, be presented to the President of the United States; if he approve, he shall sign it, but if not, he shall return it, with his objections, to that House in which it shall have originated, who shall enter the objections at large on their journal, and proceed to reconsider it."

226. Repeat that portion which relates to the second passage of a Bill, after it has been vetoed.

"If, after such reconsideration, two-thirds of that House shall agree to pass the bill, it shall be sent, together with the objections, to the other House, by which it shall likewise be reconsidered, and if approved by two-thirds of that House, it shall become a law."

227. Repeat the portion which relates to the recording of the vote.

"In all such cases the votes of both Houses shall be determined by yeas and nays, and the names of the persons voting for and against the bill shall be entered on the journal of each House, respectively."

228. Repeat that portion of Clause II. which limits the time that the President may retain a Bill.

"If any bill shall not be returned by the President within ten days (Sundays excepted,) after it shall have been presented to him, the same shall be a law, in like manner as if he had signed it, unless the Congress, by their adjournment, prevent its return, in which case it shall not be a law."

229. Repeat the whole of Clause II.

CLAUSE III. "*Every order, resolution, or vote, to which the concurrence of the Senate and House of Representatives may be necessary (except on a question of adjournment), shall be presented to the President of the United States; and before the same shall take effect, shall be approved by him, or, being disapproved by him, shall be repassed by two-thirds of the Senate and House of Representatives, according to the rules and limitations prescribed in the case of a bill.*"

230. What is the object of this clause?

It extends the veto of the President to other matters besides bills.

231. To what other matters does his veto extend?

To all orders, resolutions or votes, (except on questions of adjournment,) to which the concurrence of the two Houses may be necessary.

232. What is the object of this provision?

To prevent Congress from evading the veto power, by passing a law under some other name.

233. What is the mode of proceeding in such cases?

The same as in the case of a bill.

234. In what case of joint resolutions has the President no veto power?

On a question of adjournment.

235. Repeat Clause III.

SECTION VIII. *Powers granted to Congress.*

CLAUSE I.   Congress shall have power ;

" *To lay and collect taxes, duties, imposts, and excises, to pay the debts and provide for the common defence and general welfare of the United States ; but all duties, imposts, and excises, shall be uniform throughout the United States.*"

236. To what does this clause relate?

To the power of taxation.

237. What is a tax?

Money exacted by Government from individuals, for the public service.

238. How are taxes sometimes divided?

Into direct taxes and indirect taxes.

239. What are direct taxes?

Taxes upon individuals.

240. What two kinds of direct taxes are there?

Taxes upon persons, and taxes upon property.

241 What are these two kinds of taxes called?

The former is called a personal, poll, or capitation tax ; the latter a property tax.

242. What is an indirect tax?

A tax upon the consumption of certain articles.

243. What three kinds of indirect taxes are there?

Taxes on goods imported into the country, taxes on on goods exported out of the country, and taxes on goods manufactured in the country; in other words, upon imports, exports, and manufactures.

245. What are "Imposts"?

Taxes on goods imported.

246. What are "Duties" and "Customs"?

Taxes on goods either exported or imported.

247. What are "Excises"?

Taxes on goods manufactured.

248. How are direct taxes apportioned among the several States?

In the same manner as the Representatives; that is, according to their respective numbers.

249. How are indirect taxes apportioned?

They must be uniform throughout the States.

250. What is the object of this provision?

To prevent Congress from legislating in behalf of local interests.

251. What doubt exists in regard to the meaning of his whole clause?

Whether it means that Congress has power to lay, and collect taxes, duties, imposts and excises, *and also* to pay the debts, &c.; or whether it means that Congress has power to lay and collect taxes, duties imposts and excises, *for the purpose* of paying the debts, &c.

252. What is the common interpretation?

That Congress has power to lay and collect taxes, duties, imposts and excises, *for the purpose* of paying the debts and providing for the common defence and general welfare of the United States.

253. Repeat Clause I.

CLAUSE II.   Congress shall have power;
" *To borrow money on the credit of the United States.*"

254. To what does this clause refer?

To borrowing money.

255. Is the possession of this power by Congress necessary to the existence of the National Government?

It is.

256. What would be the consequence if no such power existed?

In times of war, or great public calamities, it would be impossible to provide in time the means of meeting the public exigencies.

257. Whose credit is pledged for the payment of money borrowed by Congress?

The credit of the whole United States.

258. Repeat Clause II.

CLAUSE III.   Congress shall have power;
" *To regulate commerce with foreign nations, and among the several States, and with the Indian tribes.*"

259. To what does Clause III. relate?

To the regulation of commerce.

260 How was commerce regulated under the Confederation?

The Continental Congress, under the Confederation had no power to regulate commerce, but it was left to the management of each particular State.

261 What was the consequence of that arrangement?

The foreign commerce of the States was almost en-

tirely destroyed, and the conflicting claims of the
several States had brought them to the brink of a
civil war.

262. What is to be understood by regulating Commerce?

Prescribing the rules by which Commerce is to be
governed.

263. What two things are included in the general idea of Commerce?

Traffic, or the interchange of commodities; and
commercial intercourse, or navigation.

264. What are some of the ways in which Congress may regulate
Commerce?

By passing laws for the coasting trade and fisheries,
and for the government of seamen on board of Ame
rican ships; by making quarantine and pilotage laws;
by constructing lighthouses; by surveying the coast
and harbours; by imposing duties upon articles imported or exported; by prohibiting commerce with
particular nations; by designating particular ports
of entry; and in various other ways.

265. To whom belonged the power of regulating Commerce
with the Indian tribes, before the Revolution?

To the King.

266. To whom does it now belong?

To Congress.

267. Repeat Clause III.

CLAUSE IV.   Congress shall have power;
" *To establish a uniform rule of naturalization, and
uniform laws on the subject of bankruptcies, throughout
the United States.*"

268. To what does the first part of this clause relate?

To naturalizing foreigners.

269. What is meant by naturalizing foreigners?

Giving them the rights of citizenship.

270. Why could not this power be left with the States?

There would then be no uniformity on the subject.

271. What would be the objection to that?

A citizen of one State is, by the Constitution, entitled to all the rights of citizenship in every other State; consequently, one State might, by its naturalization laws, invade the rights and privileges of all the rest.

272. According to the rule of naturalization adopted by Congress, how long must a foreigner live in the country before he can become a citizen?

At least five years.

273. To what does the latter part of this clause relate?

To Bankruptcy.

274. What should be the object of bankrupt and insolvent laws, in regard to creditors?

To secure to creditors the full surrender and equitable distribution of the insolvent debtor's effects.

275. What should be their object in regard to unfortunate debtors?

To secure to them, after such a surrender, a legal discharge from their creditors.

276. What is the effect of giving to creditors the power to imprison a debtor, or to seize upon his future earnings?

It either paralyzes all exertion, or leads to fraudulent means to secrete property afterwards acquired.

277. Does the discharge of a debtor from the power of his creditors release him from all obligation to pay his debts?

It does not. He is still bound in honour and conscience to pay his debts, if in subsequent business he shall acquire the means.

278. Is there any uniform law of bankruptcy now existing in the United States?

There is.   Congress passed such a law in the year 1801, which was repealed in 1803. Another was passed in 1842, which was repealed in 1843. In 1866 a new Bankrupt Law was passed, and is now in force.

279. Repeat Clause IV.

CLAUSE V. Congress shall have power;
" *To coin money, regulate the value thereof, and of foreign coin, and fix the standard of weights and measures.*"

280. To what does the first part of this clause refer ?
To the power of coinage.

281. To whom is this power entrusted?
To Congress exclusively.

282. What would be the consequence of giving to each State the power to coin money ?
There would be no uniformity in the weight or value of money, and the circulation of base or counterfeit coin would be very much increased.

283. To what does the latter part of this clause relate ?
To fixing the standard of weights and measures.

284. Repeat Clause V.

CLAUSE VI. Congress shall have power;
" *To provide for the punishment of counterfeiting the securities and current coin of the United States.*"

285. What is the object of this provision ?
To render more efficient the powers of coinage and of borrowing money.

286. Repeat Clause VI.

CLAUSE VII.   Congress shall have power ;
" *To establish post offices and post roads.*"

287. What are some of the advantages which result from the exercise of this power?

It enables both individuals and the government to transmit intelligence, to make remittances of money, and to transact various important branches of business with a degree of promptitude, regularity and economy, that would be entirely impracticable in any other way.

CLAUSE VIII. Congress shall have power;

" *To promote the progress of science and useful arts by securing, for limited times, to authors and inventors the exclusive right to their respective writings and discoveries.*"

288. What is the object of this clause?

To secure the rights of authors and inventors.

289. How long may a person, under the existing laws of the United States, have the exclusive right to publish any book of which he is the author?

Twenty-eight years.

290. What is this privilege called?

A copyright.

291. May a copyright be renewed?

It may, for an additional period of fourteen years.

292. How long may a person have the exclusive right to manufacture and sell any machine of which he is the inventor?

Fourteen years.

293. What is this privilege called?

A patent right.

294. Repeat Clause VIII.

CLAUSE IX. Congress shall have power;

" *To constitute tribunals inferior to the Supreme Court.*"

N. B. This subject will be considered more fully under the head of the Judicial Department.

CLAUSE X. Congress shall have power ;
*" To define and punish piracies and felonies committed
on the high seas, and offences against the law of nations."*

295. What is Piracy ?
Robbery at sea.

296. What is the punishment for Piracy, or felony committed
on the high seas?
Death.

297. When is an action said to have been done upon the " high
seas ?"
When it is done beyond low water mark.

298. Why is Congress particularly charged with the punishment
of offences against the law of nations ?
Because the United States are responsible to foreign
nations for the conduct of American citizens at sea.

299. Repeat Clause X.

CLAUSE XI. Congress shall have power ;
*" To declare war, grant letters of marque and reprisal,
and make rules concerning captures on land and water."*

300. With whom is the right of declaring war vested in monarchical governments ?
With the Executive.

301. Why is this inexpedient ?
The people, who have to bear the burden of war,
ought to have as direct a voice as possible in deciding
whether or not to declare war.

302. What are Letters of Marque and Reprisal ?
Commissions granted to private persons to capture
the property of citizens of another nation.

303. What is a person so commissioned called ?
A Privateer.

304 When are Letters of Marque and Reprisal generally issued ?

In time of war.

305 Are they ever granted at other times?

Sometimes an individual, for whom no redress of grievances can be obtained from a foreign nation, is permitted by his own government to make reprisa' upon the property of subjects of that nation to the ex tent of his injury.

306. Repeat Clause XI.

CLAUSE XII. Congress shall have power;

"To raise and support armies; but no appropriation of money to that use shall be for a longer term than two years."

307. Should the power of raising armies always be connectea with that of declaring war?

It should.

308. How was it under the Articles of Confederation?

Congress had the right to declare war, but the States only could raise troops.

309. What was the consequence of a similar arrangement during the Revolutionary War?

Great expense, delay, and inefficiency.

310. Why is Congress not allowed to make any appropriation for the support of the army for more than two years?

To prevent the maintenance of a standing army in time of peace, without the continued consent of the people.

311. How often are the appropriations for the army actually made?

Every year.

312. What is all the legislation that would be necessary at any time to disband the army?

All that would be necessary for this purpose would

be for the Representatives of the people to omit providing for its support in the annual appropriation bill.

313. Repeat Clause XII.

CLAUSE XIII. Congress shall have power;
"*To provide and maintain a navy.*"

314. What may be remarked of the general object of this clause?
Its general object is the same as that relating to the Army.

315. What may be remarked of the danger of maintaining a large naval force?
A Navy is always considered less dangerous to the liberties of a country than a standing Army.

CLAUSE XIV. Congress shall have power;
" *To make rules for the government and regulation of the land and naval forces.*"

CLAUSE XV. Congress shall have power;
" *To provide for calling forth the militia to execute the laws of the Union, suppress insurrections, and repel invasions.*"

316. Why is Congress intrusted with this power to call out the militia?
To enable them to discharge the duty of maintaining the public peace.

317. What would be the alternative if this power was not granted?
It would be necessary to maintain a standing army.

318. What is to be observed of the limitation of this power?
Congress is not limited either in regard to the time of service, or the place of operation.

319. What is inferred from the use of the word "*provide?*"
Congress may instruct the President to judge of the

exigency, and to call out the militia, in certain con
tingencies, during the recess of Congress.

320. Repeat Clause XV.

CLAUSE XVI. Congress shall have power;

"*To provide for organizing, arming, and disciplining
the militia, and for governing such part of them as may
be employed in the service of the United States; reserv-
ing to the States respectively, the appointment of the
officers, and the authority of training the militia, according to the discipline prescribed by Congress.*"

321. Why is it left to the State Governments to train the Militia
and appoint the officers?

The Militia is considered as intended mainly for the
maintenance of the State Governments, to be called
out by the General Government only in certain specia
exigencies.

322. Why is the organization and mode of discipline left to be
prescribed by Congress?

To secure uniformity in these respects, as well as
efficiency in case of actual service.

323. Repeat Clause XVI.

CLAUSE XVII. Congress shall have power;

" *To exercise exclusive legislation in all cases what-
soever, over such district (not exceeding ten miles square,)
as may, by cession of particular States, and the accept-
ance of Congress, become the seat of the Government of
the United States, and to exercise like authority over all
places, purchased by the consent of the legislature of the
State in which the same shall be, for the erection of forts
magazines, arsenals, dockyards, and other needful build-
ings.*"

324. To what does this clause principally relate?

To the seat of the National Government.

325. What limit is prescribed by the Constitution as to the extent of country to be occupied as the Seat of Government?

It shall not exceed ten miles square.

326. What other limitation is given?

The place selected must be ceded for that purpose by the State or States within which it lies.

327. What provision is made in regard to places occupied by the United States for forts, arsenals, dockyards, &c.?

If purchased by the consent of the State Legislature, the General Government acquires exclusive jurisdiction over them, as in the case of the Seat of Government.

328. Repeat Clause XVII.

CLAUSE XVIII. Congress shall have power;

" *To make all laws which shall be necessary and proper for carrying into execution the foregoing powers, and all other powers vested by this Constitution in the Government of the United States, or in any department or officer thereof.*"

329. How is this clause to be considered?

Merely as declaratory of what is actually implied in the other provisions of the Constitution.

330. Why was it deemed necessary to make such a declaration?

Because in the Articles of Confederation there was an express declaration to the contrary effect, that is, prohibiting Congress from the exercise of any powers not expressly granted.

331. Repeat Clause XVIII.

———

SECTION IX. *Powers denied to the United States.*

CLAUSE I. " *The migration or importation of such persons, as any of the States, now existing, shall think proper to admit, shall not be prohibited by the Congress prior to the year one thousand eight hundred and eight ; but a tax or duty may be imposed on such importation not exceeding ten dollars for each person.*"

332. To what does this clause relate ?

To the abolition of the foreign Slave Trade.

333. Were any attempts made before the American Revolution to prevent the importation of slaves into this country ?

Several of the Colonies, before the Revolution, passed laws prohibiting the importation of slaves ; but these laws were negatived by the British Government.

334. What was the earliest period fixed upon in the Constitution for putting an end to the importation of slaves ?

The year 1808.

335. What hindrance to the importation could Congress interpose, without directly prohibiting it ?

A tax of ten dollars upon every person so imported.

336. When was the importation actually prohibited ?

Congress passed a Bill in 1807, prohibiting the importation of slaves after January 1, 1808.

337. When was the importation into the British Colonies pro hibited ?

The same year, 1808.

Repeat Clause I.

CLAUSE II. " *The privilege of the writ of* habeas corpus *shall not be suspended unless when, in cases of rebellion or invasion, the public safety may require it.*"

338. What is the object of this clause ?

To prevent illegal imprisonment.

339. What remedy has a person who thinks himself illegally con fined or imprisoned ?

He petitions the judge to be brought into ope*

Court, in order that the cause of his imprisonment may be inquired into.

340. What is the meaning of the words *habeas corpus*?
" *That you have the body.*"

341. How are these words used?
The judge orders the person who holds another under confinement, to this effect: " See *that you have the body*," (produce the person in open court,) to be submitted to the decision of the judge.

342. When may Congress suspend this privilege?
In cases of rebellion and invasion.

343. Why were they prohibited from suspending it in all other cases?
To preserve the citizens of the United States from the oppressions that had been practised in Great Britain by the frequent suspension of this privilege.

344. Repeat Clause II.

CLAUSE III. ' *No bill of attainder, or* ex post facto *law, shall be passed.*"

345. What is a Bill of attainder?
A Bill passed by the Legislature, convicting a person of crimes, and punishing him therefor, without a regular trial.

346. What is the objection to a bill of attainder?
It deprives the citizen of his inalienable right of trial by jury.

347. What are *ex post facto* laws?
Laws made after the act is done.

348. What is the operation of an *ex post facto* law?
When an act has been done against which there was no law, a law may be afterwards passed, decla-

ring the act to have been a crime, and punishing it accordingly

349. Is Congress allowed to pass such laws ?

It is not.

350. Repeat Clause III.

CLAUSE IV. " *No capitation or other direct tax, shall be laid, unless in proportion to the* census *or enumeration, herein before directed to be taken.*"

351. What is the object of this clause ?

To prevent Congress from laying the burdens of government unequally upon different portions of the republic.

CLAUSE V. " *No tax or duty shall be laid on articles exported from any State. No preference shall be given by any regulation of commerce or revenue, to the ports of one State over those of another ; nor shall vessels bound to, or from, one State, be obliged to enter, clear, or pay duties, in another.*"

352. What is the object of the first part of this clause ?

To prevent Congress from injuring the interests of any one of the States.

353. How might this be done ?

By laying a tax upon the export of its staple productions.

354 What is the object of the next part of the clause ?

To prevent any preference of the ports of one State to those of another.

355. To what does the last part of the clause refer ?

To the practice, which existed previous to the Revolution, of requiring all vessels from the Colonies, no matter to what part of the world they were bound, to go by way of Great Britain, and sail to and from some British port.

356. What was the object of that system?

To throw all the commerce of the Colonies into the hands of the British.

357. What is the object of this prohibition in the Constitution?

To prevent Congress from putting the commerce of the country under the control of any particular section.

358. Repeat Clauses IV. and V.

CLAUSE VI. " No money shall be drawn from the treasury, but in consequence of appropriations made by law; and a regular statement and account of the receipts and expenditures of all public money shall be published, from time to time."

359. What is forbidden in the first part of this clause?

Drawing money from the Treasury, except in consequence of appropriations made by law.

360. What is required in the latter part of the clause?

Government is required to publish a full account of its receipts and expenditures.

361. What is the object of these provisions?

To make both the Legislature and the Executive duly responsible for the use of the public money.

362. Repeat Clause VI.

CLAUSE VII. " No title of nobility shall be granted by the United States: And no person, holding any office of profit or trust under them, shall, without the consent of the Congress, accept of any present, emolument, office, or title, of any kind whatever, from any king, prince, or foreign state."

363. Why are titles of nobility prohibited?

Because in this country all citizens have equa
lignts.

364. Why are officers of Government forbidden to receive any
present, emolument, office or title, from foreign States or Princes?

To prevent foreign governments from unduly in
fluencing our affairs.

365. R?peat Clause VII.

SECTION X. *Powers denied to the States.*

CLAUSE I. " *No State shall enter into any treaty, alliance, or confederation ; grant letters of marque and reprisal ; coin money ; emit bills of credit ; make anything
but gold and silver coin a tender in payment of debts,
pass any bill of attainder,* ex post facto *law, or law impairing the obligation of contracts, or grant any title of
nobility.*"

366. Why should no State be allowed to enter into any treaty,
alliance, or confederation?

. Such a privilege would conflict with the powers
granted to the General Government.

367. Why should no State be allowed to grant letters of marque
and reprisal?

Such a privilege would enable one State, at its
pleasure, to involve all the others in a general war.

368. Why should no State be allowed to coin money?

Such a privilege would lead to the introduction of a
currency exceedingly various and changeable, instead
of that simple and uniform currency which we now
have.

369. What is alluded to in the prohibition to issue bills of credit?

The currency which existed during the Revolutionary War, and which was called "Continental
money."

370. What is here meant b "Bills of Credit"?

Paper money; or promises to pay, issued by a State, in such a way, as to be used as a circulating medium.

371. Is this phrase interpreted to prohibit a State from borrowing money by giving its bonds?

It is not.

372. What fact is alluded to in the prohibition to make anything but gold and silver coin a tender for the payment of debts?

During the Revolutionary War, laws were passed requiring the people to receive the Continental money at its par value, in payment of debts.

373. What is a legal tender?

Such an offer of payment as the creditor is obliged to accept, or forfeit his claim to interest.

374. Have bills of attainder, or *ex post facto* laws, ever been passed in this country?

During the Revolutionary War, the States confiscated the property of those who espoused the cause of the mother country.

375. What instances have occurred in our history of " laws impairing the obligation of contracts "?

The laws, making the depreciated Continental money a legal tender, and various laws of the same kind, passed by the States during the Revolutionary War.

376. Are the States prohibited from making insolvent laws, discharging contracts in certain cases?

The Supreme Court has decided that the States may pass such laws in reference to *future* contracts, but not to those which are *past*.

377. Repeat the whole of Clause I.

CLAUSE II " *No State shall, without the consent of the Congress, lay any imposts or duties on imports or exports, except what may be absolutely necessary for exe-*

cuting its inspection laws; and the net produce of all duties and imposts, laid by any State on imports or exports, shall be for the use of the treasury of the United States; and all such laws shall be subject to the revision and control of the Congress. No State shall, without the consent of Congress, lay any duty on tonnage, keep troops or ships of war, in time of peace, enter into any agreement or compact with another State, or with a foreign power, or engage in war, unless actually invaded, or in such imminent danger, as will not admit of delay."

378. What is the object of the first part of this clause?

To prevent the States from making laws, interfering with the general authority of Congress, to regulate commerce.

379. What is necessary before any State can lay any imposts or duties on imports or exports?

The consent of Congress.

380. What are inspection laws?

Laws requiring certain articles, raised in a State, to be examined and approved before exportation.

381. What is the object of such laws?

To improve the quality of the articles exported.

382. What is done with the net produce of all duties laid by the States for this purpose?

It goes into the Treasury of the United States.

383. What still further limitation is put upon this power of the States?

The laws passed for this purpose are subject to the revision of Congress.

384. What would be the consequence of allowing the States to maintain troops and ships of war?

It would endanger the public safety.

385. Why should not the States be allowed to enter into compact with each other or with foreign States?

Such compacts would be incompatible with the safety of the Union.

386. In what case may the States engage in war?

When actually invaded, or in such imminent danger as will not admit of delay.

387. Repeat Clause II.

ARTICLE II. EXECUTIVE DEPARTMENT.

SECTION I. *President and Vice-President.*

CLAUSE I. " *The Executive power shall be vested in a President of the United States of America. He shall hold his office during the term of four years, and together with the Vice-President, chosen for the same term, be elected as follows:*"

388. In whom is the Executive power of the United States vested?

In the President.

389. For how long a term is the President elected?

For four years.

390. What other executive officer is chosen at the same time and for the same period?

The Vice-President.

391. How does the President's term of service compare with that of Senators and Representatives?

It is between the two; that of Senators being six years, that of Representatives two.

392. What advantage results from this arrangement?

The different departments of government are never all dissolved at the same time.

393. What evil might result from a shorter term of service?

Sudden fluctuations in the policy of the General Government.

394. What danger might be apprehended from too long a term of service?

It might tend to make the Executive independent of the will of the people.

395. Repeat Clause I.

CLAUSE II. " *Each State shall appoint, in such manner as the Legislature thereof may direct, a number of Electors, equal to the whole number of Senators and Representatives, to which the State may be entitled in the Congress: but no Senator or Representative, or person holding an office of trust or profit, under the United States, shall be appointed an Elector.*"

396. For what does this clause provide?

For the appointment of Electors, to choose the President and Vice-President.

397. How are these Electors appointed?

In such manner as the Legislature of each State may direct.

398. To how many Electors is each State entitled?

To as many as the whole number of Senators and Representatives to which the State may be entitled in Congress.

399. What persons are disqualified from being appointed Electors?

Senators, Representatives, and all persons holding any office of trust or profit under the United States.

400. Repeat Clause II.

[CLAUSE III. " The Electors shall meet in their respective States, and vote by ballot for two persons, of whom one, at least, shall not be an inhabitant of the same State with themselves. And they shall make a list of all the persons voted for, and of the number of votes for each; which list they shall sign and certify, and transmit, sealed, to the seat of the government of the United States, directed to the President of the Senate. The President of the Senate shall, in the presence of the Senate and House of Representatives, open all the candidates, and the votes shall then be counted. The person having the greatest number of votes shall be the President, if such number be a majority of the whole number of Electors appointed; and if there be more than one, who have such majority, and have an equal number of votes, then the House of Representatives shall immediately choose, by ballot, one of them for President; and if no person have a majority, then, from the five highest on the list, the said House shall, in like manner, choose the President. But in choosing the President, the votes shall be taken by States, the representation from each State having one vote; a quorum for this purpose, shall consist of a member or members from two-thirds of the States, and a majority of all the States shall be necessary to a choice. In every case, after the choice of the President, the person having the greatest number of votes of the Electors shall be the Vice-President. But if there should remain two or more who have equal votes, the Senate shall choose from them, by ballot, the Vice-President."]

N. B. This clause has since been repealed. It is quoted here merely for reference, and not to be learned by the pupil. Instead of learning it, he should study the following, which is Article XII. of the Amendments, and which contains the present mode of electing the President and Vice-President. This Amendment is treated of here, because of its connexion with the present subject.

AMENDMENT, ARTICLE XII.

Mode of choosing the President and Vice-President.

CLAUSE I. " *The Electors shall meet in their respective States, and vote by ballot for President and Vice-President, one of whom, at least, shall not be an inhabitant of the same State with themselves ; they shall name in their ballots the person voted for as President, and in distinct ballots the person voted for as Vice-President ; and they shall make distinct lists of all persons voted for as President, and of all persons voted for as Vice-President, and of the number of votes for each, which lists they shall sign, and certify, and transmit, sealed, to the seat of the government of the United States, directed to the President of the Senate : the President of the Senate shall, in the presence of the Senate and House of Representatives, open all the certificates, and the votes shall then be counted; the person having the greatest number of votes for President shall be the President, if such number be a majority of the whole number of Electors appointed; and if no person have such majority, then, from the persons having the highest numbers, not exceeding three, on the list of those voted for as President, the House of Representatives shall choose immediately, by ballot, the President. But in choosing the President, the votes shall be taken by States, the representation from each State having one vote; a quorum for this purpose shall consist of a member or members from two-thirds of the States, and a majority of all the States shall be necessary to a choice. And if the House of Representatives shall not choose a President, whenever the right to choose shall devolve upon them, before the fourth day of March next following, then the Vice-President shall act as President, as in case of the death, or other constitutional disability, of the President."*

CLAUSE II. *" The person having the greatest number of votes as Vice-President shall be the Vice-President, if such number be a majority of the whole number of Electors appointed; and if no person have a majority, then, from the two highest numbers on the list, the Senate shall choose the Vice-President; a quorum for the purpose shall consist of two-thirds of the whole number of Senators; a majority of the whole number shall be necessary to a choice."*

CLAUSE III. *" But no person constitutionally ineligible to the office of President, shall be eligible to that of Vice-President of the United States."*

401. Where do the Electors meet?

In their respective States.

402. What is prescribed in regard to their mode of voting?

It shall be by ballot.

403. What is the object of not allowing them to select both Presi
ident and Vice-President from the same State with themse ves?

To prevent local partialities.

404. How are they required to make their ballots?

They shall name in their ballots the person voted
for as President, and in distinct ballots, the person
voted ior as Vice-President.

405. How does this differ from the former mode of balloting?

Before the amendment of the Constitution, the
Electors in each State voted for two persons as candidates for the Presidency. When the votes of all the
States were collected, the one who had the greatest
number of votes was President; the one who had the
next greatest number was Vice-President. By the
present plan, the votes for President and Vice-President are distinct.

406. What provision is made to prevent *mistake* in regard to the
result of the balloting?

The Electors shall make distinct lists of all persons
voted for as President, and of all persons voted for as
Vice-President, and of the number of votes for each.

407. What provision is made to prevent *fraud?*

The Electors shall sign, certify, and seal the lists
which contain the result of their votes.

408. Where do they send these lists?

To the Seat of Government.

409. To whom?

To the President of the Senate.

410. Repeat that part of the Clause which relates to what is done
by the Electors in each State.

" The Electors shall meet in their respective States,
and vote by ballot for President and Vice-President,
one of whom, at least, shall not be an inhabitant o

the same State with themselves; they shall name in their ballots the person voted for as President, and in distinct ballots the person voted for as Vice-President; and they shall make distinct lists of all persons voted for as President, and of all persons voted for as Vice-President, and of the number of votes for each, which lists they shall sign, and certify, and transmit, sealed, to the seat of the Government of the United States, directed to the President of the Senate."

411. What provision is made to prevent frauds in counting the votes at the Seat of Government?

The President of the Senate shall, in the presence of the Senate and House of Representatives, open all the certificates, and the votes shall then be counted.

412. What number of Electoral votes is necessary to an election?

A majority of the whole number.

413. Why should not a person be elected who had a *plurality* of votes?

In case there were several candidates, a person might be elected by a small number of votes, against the wishes of a large majority of the people.

414. Repeat that part of the clause which relates to the counting of the votes, and the number necessary to a choice.

" The President of the Senate shall, in the presence of the Senate and House of Representatives, open all the certificates, and the votes shall then be counted; the person having the greatest number of votes for President, shall be the President, if such number be a majority of the whole number of Electors appointed."

415. What is to be done, in case no candidate has a majority of the whole number of votes?

The House of Representatives shall elect a President.

416. By ballot, or *viva voce?*

By ballot.

417. When?

Immediately.

418. How are they limited in their choice?

To the *three* candidates highest on the list.

419. How was it, in this respect, before the Amendment?

The House chose from the *five* highest.

420. In what manner shall the votes of the House be taken in choosing the President?

By States; the Representation from each State having but one vote.

421. What States are favoured by this mode of voting?

The small States. The smallest State has, in such a case, as much weight as the largest.

422. What States have the preponderance when a choice is made by the Electors?

The large States.

423. In choosing the President b ⁺ʰᵉ House, what is necessary to make a quorum of the House

A Member or Members from two-thirds of the States.

424. What number of States is necessary to a choice by the House?

A majority of all the States.

425. Repeat that part of the clause which relates to the election of President by the House.

" If no person have such majority, then, from the persons having the highest numbers, not exceeding three, on the list of those voted for as President, the House of Representatives shall choose immediately, by ballot, the President. But in choosing the President, the votes shall be taken by States, the Representation from each State having one vote; a quorum for this purpose shall consist of a member or

members from two-thirds of the States, and a majority
of all the States shall be necessary to a choice."

426. If the right of choice devolves upon the House, and they fail
immediately to choose a President, how long can this duty be
deferred ?

Not longer than the 4th of March next following.

427. Why is that day particularly named?

Because the existing President's term of office ex-
pires on that day.

428. In case the House fail to make a choice before the 4th of
March, who succeeds to the Presidency ?

The Vice-President.

429. Repeat that part of the clause which relates to the failure of
the House to choose a President.

" And if the House of Representatives shall not
choose a President, whenever the right of choice shall
devolve upon them, before the fourth day of March
next following, then the Vice-President shall act as
President, as in case of the death, or other constitutional disability of the President."

430. What number of Electoral votes is necessary to elect the
Vice-President ?

A majority of the whole number.

431. In case no one of the candidates has such a majority, how is
the Vice-President elected ?

By the Senate.

432. How is the Senate limited in its choice ?

To the *two* candidates highest on the list.

433. What constitutes a quorum of the Senate for choosing the
Vice-President ?

Two-thirds of the whole number of Senators.

434. What number of Senators is necessary to a choice ?

A majority of the whole number.

435 Does the Senate, in choosing the Vice-President, vote by States ?

It does not.

436. Repeat the clause relating to the election of Vice-President.

" The person having the greatest number of votes as Vice-President, shall be the Vice-President, if such number be a majority of the whole number of electors appointed ; and if no person have a majority, then, from the two highest numbers on the list, the Senate shall choose the Vice-President ; a quorum for the purpose shall consist of two-thirds of the whole number of Senators ; a majority of the whole number shall be necessary to a choice."

437. Why are the same qualifications required of the Vice-President as of the President ?

Because, in certain cases, the Vice-President succeeds to the office of President.

438. Repeat the clause referring to this.

" But no person constitutionally ineligible to the office of President, shall be eligible to that of Vice-President of the United States."

439. Repeat the whole of the Amendment relating to the mode of choosing President and Vice-President.

CLAUSE IV. " *The Congress may determine the time of choosing the Electors, and the day on which they shall give their votes; which day shall be the same throughout the United States.*"

440. How is the time of choosing Presidential Electors determined '

By Congress.

441 What is this choice of Electors generally called ?

The Presidental election.

442. Is the day for choosing Electors the same throughout the States ?

It is.   By act of Congress, of January 23d, 1545 the electors are to be chosen in each State on the Tuesday next after the first Monday in November.

443. How is the day on which the Electors shall vote for President and Vice-President determined ?

That also is determined by Congress.

444. Under what limitation?

That it shall be the same throughout the United States.

445. What is the object of this provision ?

To prevent fraudulent combinations.

446. Repeat Clause IV.

CLAUSE V. " *No person, except a natural-born citizen, or a citizen of the United States at the time of the adoption of this Constitution, shall be eligible to the office of President; neither shall any person be eligible to that office who shall not have attained to the age of thirty-five years, and been fourteen years a resident within the United States.*

447. To what does this clause relate ?

To the qualifications of the President.

448. Of what age must a person be, before he can be eligible to the office of President ?

Thirty-five years.

449. How long must he have been a resident in the United States ?

Fourteen years.

450. Does this exclude from the office persons who are abroad in the public service ?

It does not.

451. What is required in regard to birth ?

The candidate must be a natural born citizen.

452. What temporary exception was made to this rule ?

An exception in favour of those who were citizens at the time of the adoption of the Constitution.

453. Why was this exception then made?

From gratitude to those distinguished foreigners who had taken part with us during the Revolution.

454. Repeat Clause V.

CLAUSE VI. "*In case of the removal of the President from office, or of his death, resignation, or inability to discharge the powers and duties of the said office, the same shall devolve on the Vice-President, and the Congress may by law provide for the case of removal, death, resignation, or inability, both of the President and Vice-President, declaring what officer shall then act as President, and such officer shall act accordingly, until the disability be removed, or a President shall be elected.*"

455. When does the office of President devolve on the Vice-President?

In case of the removal of the President from office, or of his death, resignation, or inability to discharge the powers and duties of said office.

456. In case of the removal, death, resignation, or inability of both President and Vice-President, what is to be done?

Congress may, by law, provide for such a case, declaring what officer shall then act as President.

457. How long shall such officer act?

Until the disability shall be removed, or a President shall be elected.

458. Repeat Clause VI.

CLAUSE VII. "*The President shall, at stated times, receive for his services, a compensation, which shall neither be increased nor diminished during the period for which he shall have been elected, and he shall not receive within that period, any other emolument from the United States, or any of them.*"

459. Why should a compensation be granted to the President?

The expense of the office might otherwise exclude persons in moderate circumstances.

460. Why should this compensation not be increased during the continuance of a President in office?

A corrupt President might abuse the patronage of his office, in order to get such increase of emolument.

461. Why should the compensation not be diminished during the continuance of a President in office?

If Congress had the power of diminishing indefinitely the compensation of the President, it would go far to destroy his independence.

462. What other restriction is put upon the compensation of the President?

He shall not receive, within that period, any other emolument from the United States, or any of them.

463. Repeat Clause VII.

CLAUSES VIII. AND IX. " *Before he enter on the execution of his office, he shall take the following oath or affirmation: ' I do solemnly swear (or affirm), that I will faithfully execute the office of President of the United States and will, to the best of my ability, preserve, protect, and defend the Constitution of the United States.*' "

464. What must the President do before entering upon his office?

He must take an oath to perform faithfully the duties of his office.

465 What are the words of this Oath?

——

SECTION II. *Powers of the President.*

CLAUSE I. " *The President shall be commander-in chief of the army and navy of the United States, and of the militia of the several States, when called into the actual service of the United States; he may require the opinion, in writing, of the principal officer in each of the executive departments, upon any subject relating to the duties of their respective offices, and he shall have power to grant reprieves and pardons for offences against the United States, except in cases of impeachment."*

466. What military and naval command does the President hold?

He is Commander-in-chief of the Army and Navy of the United States, and of the Militia of the several States, when called into the actual service of the United States.

467. Why should the command of the Army and Navy be intrusted to the President, rather than to Congress?

Because military and naval operations require a degree of promptitude and unity, which could not be obtained in a numerous body like Congress.

468. What may the President require of the Heads of Departments?

He may require their opinion, in writing, upon any subject relating to the duties of their respective offices.

469. Has the President any pardoning power?

He has power to grant reprieves and pardons for offences against the United States, except in cases of impeachment.

470. In what manner is the pardoning power sometimes useful?

It enables the Executive, by a promise of pardon to one criminal, to detect and punish others.

471. In what case has the President no power of pardon?

In cases of impeachment.

472. Repeat Clause I.

CLAUSE II. *"He (the President) shall have power, by and*

with the advice and consent of the Senate, to make treaties, provided two-thirds of the Senators present concur ; and he shall nominate, and by and with the advice and consent of the Senate, shall appoint ambassadors, other public minis-ters, and consuls, judges of the Supreme Court, and all other officers of the United States, whose appointments are not herein otherwise provided for, and which shall be estab-lished by law : but the Congress may by law vest the ap-pointment of such inferior officers, as they think proper, in the President alone, in the courts of law, or in the heads of Departments."

473. To what does the first part of this clause relate ?

To the treaty-making power.

474. By whom are Treaties made?

By the President.

475. How is the President limited in making a Treaty ?

It must be by and with the advice and consent of the Senate.

476. How large a vote of the Senate is necessary to confirm a Treaty ?

Two-thirds of the Senators present.

477. To what does the next part of this clause relate ?

The power of appointing officers.

478. What officers are appointed by the President?

Ambassadors; other public Ministers and Consuls; Judges of the Supreme Court; and all other officers of the United States, whose appointments are not herein otherwise provided for, and which shall be es-tablished by law.

479. What limitation is put upon the appointing power of the President ?

The appointments here named must be made by and with the advice and consent of the Senate.

480. What provision is made in the Constitution, in regard to the appointment of inferior officers?

Congress may, by law, vest the appointment of such inferior officers as they think proper, in the President alone, in the Courts of Law, or in the Heads of Departments.

481. Is any provision made in the Constitution for the removal of persons from office?

There is not.

482. To whom has the power of removal been given in practice?

To the President.

483. Repeat Clause II.

CLAUSE III. " *The President shall have power to fill up all vacancies that may happen, during the recess of the Senate, by granting commissions, which shall expire at the end of their next session.*"

484. What provision is made for vacancies that may happen during the recess of the Senate?

The President has power to fill such vacancies.

485. For how long a time do the commissions thus granted continue?

They expire at the end of the next session of the Senate.

486. Why was it necessary to make some provison for temporary appointments of this sort to fill vacancies?

As these vacancies are continually occurring, by death, resignation, or otherwise, the operations of the Government would be liable to serious embarrassments, unless the Senate was kept in perpetual session.

SECTION III. *Duties of the President.*

" *He shall, from time to time, give to the Congress information of the state of the Union, and recommend to their consideration such measures as he shall judge necessary and expedient; he may, on extraordinary occasions, convene both Houses, or either of them, and in case of disagreement between them, with respect to the time of adjournment, he may adjourn them to such time as he shall think proper; he shall receive ambassadors and other public ministers; he shall take care that the laws be faithfully executed, and shall commission all the officers of the United States.*"

487. To what does the first part of this section relate?

The Messages of the President to Congress.

488. Is the duty of sending Messages to Congress optional with the President?

It is not; it is obligatory.

489. If this duty were not required of the President, what objection might possibly be made to the practice?

It might be objected to, as an improper interference of the Executive with the Legislative Department.

490. Why is it important that the President should communicate in this manner with Congress?

The Executive Department is necessarily better informed than any other Department, of the wants and resources of the nation, and of the other facts which form the appropriate basis for legislation.

491. What is the President, in his Messages to Congress, required to do?

He is required to give information of the state of the Union, and to recommend to their consideration such measures, as he shall judge necessary and expedient.

492. What provision is made in regard to Extra Sessions of Congress?

The President may, on extraordinary occasions, convene both Houses, or either of them.

493. What provision is made, in case of disagreement of the Houses, with respect to the time of adjournment?

The President may adjourn them to such time as he shall think proper.

494. To whom is given the power of receiving Ambassadors, and other public Ministers?

To the President.

495. To what danger is the exercise of this power liable?

In cases of revolution in foreign governments, or of a division of a foreign kingdom into two governments, the reception of an Ambassador or Minister from one government, might be construed by the other into an act of hostility.

496. What general duty is required of the President in regard to the laws of the United States?

He shall take care that the laws be faithfully executed.

497. What is the supreme law of the land?

The Constitution itself, and all treaties and laws made under it.

498. What is the last duty required of the President?

He is required to commission all the officers of the United States.

499. Does this include those not appointed by him?,

It does.

500. What is the propriety of this provision?

All officers of the United States should possess some proper voucher of their right to office.

501. Repeat Section III.

SECTION IV. *Impeachment of the President.*

" *The President, Vice-President, and all civil officers of the United States, shall be removed from office, on impeachment for, and conviction of, treason, bribery, or other high crimes and misdemeanours.*"

502. Who are liable to impeachment?

The President, Vice-President, and all civil officers of the United States.

503. Who are meant by officers of the United States?

Officers deriving their appointments from the National Government.

504. Does this include Members of Congress?
It does not.

505. What officers of the United States are there besides civil officers?

· Military and Naval officers.

506. Are the officers of the Army and Navy liable to impeachment?

They are not.

507. Who are the persons chiefly meant, besides the President and Vice-President?

Heads of Departments; Judges of the Supreme Court; Marshals, Collectors, District Attorneys, &c.

508. For what offences are these officers liable to impeachment?

For treason, bribery, or other high crimes and misdemeanours.

509. What is the extent of the penalty in cases of impeachment?

Removal from office, and disqualification to hold office in future.

510 Repeat Section IV.

ARTICLE III. Judicial Department.

Section I. *United States Courts.*

" *The Judicial power of the United States shall be vested in one Supreme Court, and in such inferior courts as the Congress may, from time to time, ordain and establish. The judges, both of the Supreme and inferior courts, shall hold their offices during good behaviour, and shall, at stated times, receive for their services a compensation, which shall not be diminished during their continuance in office.*

511. Where is the Judicial power of the United States vested?

In one Supreme Court, and such other courts as Congress may from time to time establish.

512. Has Government any discretion in regard to the establishment of a Supreme Court?

It has not. The establishment of one Supreme Court is positively required.

513. Why is a Supreme Court absolutely essential?

To insure uniformity in the interpretation of the laws.

514. What discretion has Congress in the matter?

Congress has the power of deciding whether any inferior Courts shall be established.

515. What are the inferior Courts, established by Congress, called?

District Courts, and Circuit Courts.

516. How many of these Courts have been established by Congress?

Forty-two District Courts, and nine Circuit Courts.

517. How are the Judges of all the United States Courts appointed?

By the President, by and with the advice and consent of the Senate.

518. What is their tenure of office?

During good behaviour.

519. Why is this considered better than appointing them for term of years?

It makes them more independent in their decisions.

520. What provision is made in regard to their compensation?

They shall at stated times receive for their services, a compensation, which shall not be diminished during their continuance in office.

521. Why is Congress not allowed to diminish a Judge's salary during his continuance in office?

Such a power would enable Congress to overawe the Judges.

522. Are the Judges entirely irresponsible?

They may be impeached for misconduct.

523. Repeat Section I.

SECTION II. *Jurisdiction of the United States Courts.*

CLAUSE I. "*The Judicial power shall extend to all cases, in law and equity, arising under this Constitution, the laws of the United States, and treaties made, or which shall be made, under their authority; to all cases affecting ambassadors, other public ministers, and consuls; to all cases of admiralty and maritime jurisdiction; to controversies to which the United States shall be a party; to controversies between two or more States, between a State and citizens of another State, between citizens of different States, between citizens of the same State, claiming lands under grants of different States, and between a State, or the citizens thereof, and foreign States, citizens or subjects.*"

524. To what does this clause relate?

To the extent of the jurisdiction of the United States Courts.

525. Are the cases over which they exercise jurisdiction numerous?

They are.

526. What is the first class of cases which may be brought before them?

Cases arising under the Constitution and Laws of the United States, and Treaties made by them.

527. Why should the United States Courts have the power of judging in all such cases?

Because the Judicial power should always be co-extensive with the Legislative and Executive powers.

528. What is the second class of cases which may be brought before the United States Courts?

Cases affecting Ambassadors, other public Ministers, and Consuls.

529. To what laws are foreign ministers amenable?

To the law of nations, and the laws of the State from which they are sent.

530. Why are public ministers not subject to the particular laws of the State or Nation to which they are sent?

Because they are the immediate representatives of the national sovereignty, which owes no subjection to foreign States.

531. Why should the National Courts alone have jurisdiction in cases relating to foreign ministers?

Because such cases always involve questions of national interest.

532. What is the third class of cases which may be brought before the United States Courts?

Cases of admiralty and maritime jurisdiction.

533. In what two ways may these cases arise?

They may arise either out of acts done at sea, or out of rights claimed under the laws of commerce.

534. Why should acts done at sea be tried solely by the National Courts?

Because such acts involve questions of international law.

535. Why should rights claimed under the laws of commerce be tried solely by the National Courts?

Because the regulation of commerce is given exclusively to the General Government.

536. What is the fourth class of cases which may come before the United States Courts?

Controversies to which the United States shall be a party.

537. What would be the consequence of not allowing the General Government to sue in its own courts?

The United States would be compelled to sue for their rights through the State tribunals, and consequently become subject to State jurisdiction.

538. What is the fifth class of cases which may come before the United States Courts?

All cases in which the parties belong to different States, or claim under laws of different States.

539. Enumerate in order the controversies which may arise from this cause.

1. Between two or more States. 2. Between a State, and citizens of another State. 3. Between citizens of different States. 4. Between citizens of the same State, claiming lands under grants of different States. 5. Between a State or its citizens, and foreign States, citizens or subjects.

540. Why should these controversaries be decided by the National Courts, and not by the State Courts?

Because the several States would naturally be inclined to favour themselves, and their own citizens.

541. What would be the consequence of not having some common and impartial umpire to decide such cases?

Dissensions among the States, and collisions with foreign States.

542. When is a State a party in a suit?

Only when it is named as such on the record.

543. Can a suit be brought against a State by a private citizen?

It could, as the Constitution was at first. An amendment was afterwards adopted, to prevent this.

AMENDMENT, ARTICLE XI.

" *The judicial power of the United States shall not be construed to extend to any suit in law or equity, commenced or prosecuted against one of the United States by citizens of another State, or by citizens or subjects of any foreign State.*"

544. Why was this amendment adopted?

Because it was thought derogatory to State sovereignty, to allow a State to be sued by a private citizen.

CLAUSE II. "*In all cases affecting ambassadors, other public ministers, and consuls, and those in which a State shall be a party, the Supreme Court shall have original jurisdiction. In all the other cases before mentioned, the Supreme Court shall have appellate jurisdiction, both as to law and fact, with such exceptions, and under such regulations, as the Congress shall make.*"

545. To what does this clause relate?

To the jurisdiction of the Supreme Court.

546. What two kinds of jurisdiction has the Supreme Court?

Original and Appellate.

547. What is *original* jurisdiction?

The right to decide a case which has been before no lower Court previously.

548. What is *appellate* jurisdiction?

The right to decide a case which is brought up by appeal from a lower Court.

549. In what cases only may the Supreme Court have original jurisdiction?

In all cases affecting ambassadors, other public ministers, and consuls, and those in which a State shall be a party.

550. What is the character of its jurisdiction in all the other cases to which the judicial power of the United States extend?

In all the other cases before mentioned, the Supreme Court shall have appellate jurisdiction, both as to law and fact, with such exceptions, and under such regulations as the Congress shall make.

551. Repeat Clause II.

CLAUSE III. " *The trial of all crimes, except in cases of impeachment, shall be by jury; and such trial shall he held in the State where the said crimes shall have been committed; but when not committed within any State, the trial shall be at such place, or places, as the Congress may by law have directed.*"

552. To what does the first part of this clause relate?
The *mode* of trial.

553. What mode of trying crimes is required?
Trial by jury.

554. What is the only exception to this rule?
The case of impeachment.

555. How has the right of trial by jury ever been regarded in this country?

As the greatest safeguard for personal liberty.

556. To what does the latter part of the clause relate?

The *place* of trial.

557. Where shall the trial of crimes be held?

In the State where said crimes shall have been committed.

558. What is the object of this provision?

To prevent the accused from being subjected to un-necessary expense and difficulty in procuring testi-mony, and to secure to him all the advantage of being tried where the facts are most likely to be known.

559. Where are crimes to be tried which are committed at sea, or not within the jurisdiction of any State?

At such place, or places, as Congress may by law have directed.

560. Repeat Clause III.

Section III. *Treason.*

Clause I. "*Treason against the United States shall consist only in levying war against them, or in adhering to their enemies, giving them aid and comfort. No person shall be convicted of treason, unless on the testi-mony of two witnesses to the same overt act, or on con-fession in open court.*"

561. What does the first part of this clause contain?

A definition of treason.

562. In what does treason against the United States consist?

In levying war against them, or in adhering to their enemies, giving them aid and comfort.

563. Why was it thought necessary so particularly to define this crime?

Because, in times of political excitement, acts of a much less heinous character have often been exag-gerated and construed into the crime of treason.

564. To what does the latter part of this clause relate?

The proof of treason.

565. What is necessary to convict a person of treason?

The testimony of two witnesses to the same overt act, or confession in open court.

566. Why is the testimony of two witnesses thought necessary?

To protect the accused party against misrepresentation.

567. Why is there more danger of misrepresentation in this, than in other crimes?

Because the charge of treason is generally made by interested partisans, and in times of great political excitement.

568. Why is it required that confession of treason, in order to be valid proof of guilt, should be made in open court?

To protect the accused party against being ruined by hasty and unguarded expressions, and against being incorrectly reported.

569. How is treason to be regarded?

As the worst crime against society that can be committed.

570. Repeat Clause I.

CLAUSE II. " *The Congress shall have power to declare the punishment of treason, but no attainder of treason shall work corruption of blood, or forfeiture, except during the life of the person attainted.*"

571. To what does this clause relate?

The punishment of treason.

572. What provision is made in regard to the punishment of treason?

It is left to Congress to declare what shall be the punishment of treason.

573. What is the punishment of treason, by the common law of England?

The traitor is to be taken to the gallows on a nurdle, hung by the neck, cut down alive, his entrails taken out and burned while he is yet alive, his head cut off, and his body quartered; beside the forfeiture of his estate and the corruption of his blood.

574. What has Congress declared to be the punishment for treason against the United States?

Death by hanging.

575. How are Congress limited in declaring the punishment of treason?

No attainder of treason shall work corruption of blood, or forfeiture, except during the life of the person attainted.

576. What is meant by an attainder of treason?

Conviction of the crime of treason.

577. What is meant by corruption of blood?

One, whose blood is corrupted, cannot inherit property from others, nor transmit an inheritance to his children; his blood ceases to have any inheritable qualities.

578. How far may Congress declare an estate forfeited?

Only during the life of the traitor.

579. Repeat Clause II.

ARTICLE IV.

SECTION I. *State Records.*

" *Full faith and credit shall be given in each State to the public acts, records, and judicial proceedings, of every other State. And the Congress may, by general laws, prescribe the manner in which such acts, records, and proceedings, shall be proved and the effect thereof.*"

580. How shall the public acts, records, and judicial proceedings of one State be regarded?

Full faith and credit shall be given to them in every other State.

581. To whom is it left to prescribe the manner in which such acts, records, and proceedings, shall be proved?

To Congress.

582. What else may Congress prescribe?

The effect of such acts, records and proceedings.

583. What would be the consequence of not having some provision of this sort?

When a legal investigation and decision had been made in one State, it might be necessary to repeat the same in every State to which the parties should go.

584. Repeat Section I.

Section II. *Privileges of Citizens, &c.*

Clause I. "*The citizens of each State shall be entitled to all privileges and immunities of citizens in the several States.*"

585. What is the object of this provision?

To prevent the States from giving unjust preferences to their own citizens.

586. What is the effect of such preferences?

Alienation and discontents.

587. Repeat Clause I.

Clause II. "*A person charged in any State with treason, felony, or other crime, who shall flee from justice, and be found in another State, shall, on demand of the executive authority of the State from which he fled, be delivered up, to be removed to the State having jurisdiction of the crime.*"

588. To what does this clause relate?

To the restoration of fugitive criminals.

589. If a person, charged in any State with treason, felony, or other crime, flee from justice, and be found in another State, who has the right to claim him?

The Executive authority of the State from which he may have fled.

590. What shall be done in such a case?

He shall be delivered up, to be removed to the State having jurisdiction of the crime.

591. Repeat Clause II.

CLAUSE III. " *No person held to service or labour in one State, under the laws thereof, escaping into another, shall, in consequence of any law or regulation therein, be discharged from such service or labour, but shall be delivered up on claim of the party to whom such service or labour may be due.*"

592. To what does this clause relate?

To the restoration of persons held to service or labour.

593. If a person held to service or labour in one State, under the laws thereof, escape into another, can such other State, by any law or regulation, discharge said person from his service or labour?

It cannot.

594. What shall be done in such a case?

The person shall be delivered up, on the claim of the party to whom such service or labour may be due.

595. Repeat Clause III.

SECTION III. *New States and Territories.*

CLAUSE I. " *New States may be admitted by the Congress into this Union; but no new State shall be formed, or erected, within the jurisdiction of any other State; nor any State be formed, by the junction of two or more States or parts of States, without the consent of the legislatures of the States concerned, as well as of the Congress.*"

596. To what does this clause relate?

The admission of new States into the Union.

597. What Department of Government has the power of admitting new States into the Union?

Congress.

598. In what two cases is this power denied to Congress?

When a new State is to be formed within the jurisdiction of any other State, or by the junction of two or more States, or parts of States.

599. What is necessary in such a case?

The consent of the States concerned, as well as of Congress.

600. Repeat Clause I.

CLAUSE II. " *The Congress shall have power to dispose of and make all needful rules and regulations respecting the territory, or other property, belonging to the United States; and nothing in this Constitution shall be so construed as to prejudice any claims of the United States, or of any particular State.*"

601. To what does this clause relate?

To the government of the Territories of the United States.

602. What power is given to Congress in this respect?

Congress shall have power to dispose of, and make all needful rules and regulations respecting, the territory, or other property, belonging to the United States.

603. What limitation is put upon this power of Congress over the Territories?

Nothing in this Constitution shall be so construed as to prejudice any claims of the United States, or of any particular State.

604. What was the cause of inserting this limitation?

At the time of the adoption of the Constitution, there were in the Western Territory certain contested titles, which, however, have since been settled.

605. Repeat Clause II.

———

Section IV. *Guarantee to the States.*

" *The United States shall guaranty to every State in this Union a republican form of government, and shall protect each of them against invasion; and, on application of the legislature, or of the executive (when the legislature cannot be convened), against domestic violence.*"

606. What shall the United States guaranty to every State in this Union?

A republican form of government.

607. What would be the consequence of one State adopting a monarchical form of government?

It might endanger the liberties of the other States.

608. For whom is this guarantee principally intended?

For the *people* of each State, to secure them against the anti-republican machinations of demagogues.

609. What do the United States further undertake?

To protect each of the States against invasion.

610. What is the last thing, mentioned in this clause, which the United States undertake?

To protect each of the States against domestic violence.

611. To what does this relate?

To the case of domestic insurrections or riots.

612. What is necessary, in such a case, to obtain the assistance of the United States?

An application of the Legislature of the State, or if they cannot be convened, of the Executive.

613. Repeat Section IV.

ARTICLE V. POWER OF AMENDMENT.

" *The Congress, whenever two-thirds of both Houses shall deem it necessary, shall propose amendments to this Constitution, or, on the application of the legislatures of two-thirds of the several States, shall call a convention for proposing amendments, which, in either case, shall be valid to all intents and purposes, as part of this Constitution, when ratified by the legislatures of three-fourths of the several States, or by conventions in three-fourths thereof, as the one or the other mode of ratification may be proposed by the Congress; Provided, that no amendment, which may be made prior to the year one thousand eight hundred and eight, shall, in any manner, affect the first and fourth clauses in the ninth section of the first article; and that no State, without its consent, shall be deprived of its equal suffrage in the Senate.*"

614. For what does this article provide?

The mode of making amendments to the Constitution.

615. Why was it thought necessary to provide for amending the Constitution?

The Constitution of the United States was an experiment in the history of nations, and its practical operation could not with certainty be foreseen.

616. What would be the consequence of having a fixed Constitution, without any peaceable means of amendment?

In case any of its provisions worked badly, they would either be silently neglected, or the Constitution itself broken up by a revolution.

617. What should be guarded against in providing for amendments?

The mode of making an amendment should not be so easy as to lead to changes without serious cause, or proper deliberation.

618. In what two ways may amendments be proposed?

By Congress, or by a Convention called for the purpose.

619. When may Congress by itself propose amendments?

Whenever two-thirds of both Houses deem it necessary.

620. When shall Congress call a Convention for proposing amendments?

On application of the Legislatures of two-thirds of the several States.

621. When an amendment has been proposed by Congress, or by a Convention, in how many ways may it be ratified?

In two ways.

622. What is the first mode of ratifying a proposed amendment?

By the State Legislatures.

623. What is the other mode?

By Conventions in the States, called for the purpose.

624. What proportion of the States must, in one of these ways ratify an amendment before it can be adopted?

Three-fourths.

625. How is the mode of ratification in any particular case determined?

By Congress.

626 What is the effect of an amendment when thus proposed and ratified?

It shall be valid, to all intents and purposes, as a part of the Constitution.

627. What *temporary* limitation was made to the power of amendment?

No amendment, which might be made prior to

1808, should, in any manner, affect the first and fourth Clauses, in the Ninth Section of Article I.

628. To what does the first of these clauses relate?

To the importation of slaves.

629. To what does the other clause relate?

To the apportionment of taxes.

630. What *permanent* limitation was made to the power of amendment?

No State, without its consent, shall be deprived of its equal suffrage in the Senate.

631. How many amendments to the Constitution have already been proposed and ratified?

Twelve.

632. Repeat Article V.

———

ARTICLE VI. Public Debt, Supremacy of the Constitution, Oath of Office, Religious Test.

Clause I. "*All debts contracted, and engagements entered into, before the adoption of this Constitution, shall be as valid against the United States, under this Constitution, as under the Confederation.*"

633. To what does this clause relate?

To the assumption by the United States of the debts contracted under the Confederation.

634. What is the acknowledged law of nations on this subject?

The obligation of a national debt continues, notwithstanding any changes in its form of government.

635. Why was it deemed advisable, in adopting the Constitution, to make a formal declaration on the subject?

To allay any apprehensions of the public creditors.

636. Repeat Clause I.

CLAUSE II. " *This Constitution, and the laws of the United States which shall be made in pursuance thereof, and all treaties made, or which shall be made, under the authority of the United States, shall be the supreme law of the land ; and the judges in every State shall be bound thereby, anything in the Constitution or laws of any State to the contrary notwithstanding.*"

637. What is declared in regard to the Constitution, and the Laws and Treaties made under it by the United States ?

They are declared to be the supreme law of the land.

638. What provision is made in the latter part of the clause to secure this supremacy ?

The Judges in every State are bound by them, anything in the Constitution or laws of any State to the contrary notwithstanding.

639. Repeat Clause II.

CLAUSE III. " *The Senators and Representatives before mentioned, and the members of the several State legislatures, and all executive and judicial officers, both of the United States, and of the several States, shall be bound, by oath or affirmation, to support this Constitution ; but no religious test shall ever be required as a qualification to any office or public trust under the United States.*"

640. Who are required to bind themselves by oath or affirmation to support the Constitution of the United States ?

The Senators and Representatives, the members of tne several State Legislatures, and all Executive and Judicial officers, both of the United States, and of the several States.

641. Why are the legislators and officers of the several States required to bind themselves to support the Constitution of the United States ?

Because the State Governments have a necessary

and important agency in carrying the Constitution of the United States into effect.

642. Give an example in which the action of the State Government is necessary to the operations of the National Government.

The election of United States Senators depends, in all cases, upon the action of the State Legislatures.

643. What prohibition is made in regard to religious tests?

No religious test shall ever be required as a qualification to any office or public trust under the United States.

———

ARTICLE VII. RATIFICATION OF THE CONSTITUTION.

"*The ratification of the Conventions of nine States shall be sufficient for the establishment of this Constitution between the States so ratifying the same.*"

644. What was necessary for the establishment of the Constitution?

Its ratification by nine of the States.

645. Would its ratification by only nine States have made it obligatory upon the four other States?

It would not.

646. On whom would it have been obligatory in such a case?

Only upon the States so ratifying it.

647. By how many of the States was it at first ratified?

By eleven.

648. Which of the States did not adopt the Constitution till after it had gone into operation?

Rhode Island and North Carolina.

AMENDMENTS TO THE CONSTITUTION.

N. B. The first Twelve Amendments were adopted in a body, immediately after the Constitution went into effect. The first ten were in the nature of a supplement, or Bill of Rights; the eleventh and twelfth were alterations.

ARTICLE I. FREEDOM OF RELIGION, &C.—"*Congress shall make no law respecting an establishment of religion, or prohibiting the free exercise thereof, or abridging the freedom of speech, or of the press; or the right of the people peaceably to assemble, and to petition the government for a redress of grievances.*"

655. What is the first prohibition upon Congress in reference to the subject of religion?

Congress shall make no law respecting an establishment of religion.

656. What other restriction is put upon Congress in regard to religion?

It shall make no law prohibiting the free exercise thereof.

657. How is Congress restricted in regard to the freedom of speech, and of the press?

It shall make no law abridging the same.

658. How is Congress restricted in regard to the right of petition?

It shall make no law abridging the right of the people peaceably to assemble, and to petition the Government for a redress of grievances.

ARTICLE II. RIGHT TO BEAR ARMS.—"*A well regulated militia being necessary to the security of a free State, the right of the people to keep and bear arms shall not be infringed.*"

659. What is here declared of a well regulated militia?

It is declared to be necessary to the security of a free State.

660. What are some of the obvious advantages of maintaining the militia?

A certain amount of military organization among the people, and a large quantity of arms always in their hands.

ARTICLE III. QUARTERING SOLDIERS ON CITIZENS.—"*No soldier shall, in time of peace, be quartered in any house, without the consent of the owner; nor, in time of war, but in a manner to be prescribed by law.*"

661. From what did this provision originate?

From the custom which has often prevailed in times of violence, of billeting soldiers upon private citizens, without regard to the rights or the convenience of the latter.

ARTICLE IV. Search Warrants.—" *The right of the people to be secure in their persons, houses, papers and effects, against unreasonable searches and seizures, shall not be violated; and no warrants shall issue, but upon probable cause, supported by oath or affirmation, and particularly describing the place to be searched, and the persons or things to be seized.*"

662. What right is it declared in this article shall not be violated?

The right of the people to be secure in their persons, houses, papers and effects, against unreasonable searches and seizures.

663. What is the only condition upon which warrants can issue?

No warrants shall issue, but upon probable cause, supported by oath or affirmation, and particularly describing the place to be searched, and the person or things to be seized.

ARTICLE V. Trial for Crime, &c.—" *No person shall be held to answer for a capital, or otherwise infamous crime, unless on a presentment or indictment of a grand jury, except in cases arising in the land or naval forces, or in the militia, when in actual service, in time of war, or public danger; nor shall any person be subject, for the same offence, to be twice put in jeopardy of life or limb; nor shall be compelled, in any criminal case, to be a witness against himself, nor be deprived of life, liberty, or property, without due process of law; nor shall private property be taken for public use, without just compensation.*"

664. What process is necessary before a person can be held to answer for a capital, or otherwise infamous crime?

A presentment or indictment of a Grand Jury.

665. What class of crimes is exempt from this mode of proceeding?

Cases arising in the land or naval forces.

666. How are such cases always tried?

By Courts-Martial.

667. When are offences in the militia tried by a Court-Martial?

Only when in actual service, in time of war or public danger.

668. Can a person who has been convicted or acquitted, be tried a second time for the same offence?

No person shall be subject for the same offence to be twice put in jeopardy of life or limb.

669. Can a person be obliged to testify against himself?

No person shall be compelled, in any criminal case, to be a witness against himself.

670. What is the next provision?

No person shall be deprived of life, liberty, or property, without due process of law.

671. What is the last provision?

Nor shall private property be taken for public use, without just compensation.

ARTICLE VI. Rights of Accused Persons.—" *In all criminal prosecutions, the accused shall enjoy the right to a speedy and public trial, by an impartial jury of the State and district wherein the crime shall have been committed, which district shall have been previously ascertained by law, and to be informed of the nature and cause of the accusation; to be confronted with the witnesses against him; to have compulsory process for obtaining witnesses in his favour; and to have the assistance of counsel for his defence."*

672. In all criminal prosecutions, what right shall the accused enjoy?
The right to a speedy and a public trial.

673. By whom shall the accused be tried?
By an impartial jury of the State and district wherein the crime shall have been committed.

674. What provision is made in regard to the district in which he shall be tried?
It must be in some district previously ascertained by law.

675. Of what has the accused the right to be informed?
Of the nature and cause of the accusation.

676. What right has he in regard to the witnesses against him?
The right to be confronted with them.

677. What right is secured in regard to testimony and counsel?
The right to have compulsory process for obtaining witnesses in his favour, and to have the assistance of counsel for his defence.

ARTICLE VII. Suits at Common Law.—*" In suits at common law, where the value in controversy shall exceed twenty dollars, the right of trial by jury shall be preserved; and no fact, tried by a jury, shall be otherwise re-examined in any court of the United States, than according to the rules of the common law."*

ARTICLE VIII. Excessive Bail.—*" Excessive bail shall not be required, nor excessive fines imposed, nor cruel and unusual punishment inflicted."*

ARTICLE IX. Reserved Rights.—*" The enumeration in the Constitution of certain rights shall not be construed to deny or disparage others retained by the people."*

ARTICLE X. Reserved Powers.—*" The powers not granted to the United States by the Constitution nor prohibited by it to the States, are reserved to the States respectively, or to the people."*

Article XI. being an amendment limiting in a certain case the jurisdiction of the Judiciary, was treated of under that head, page 83.
Article XII. being an amendment in regard to the mode of electing President and Vice President, was treated of under the head of the Executive Department, p. 63.

ARTICLE XIII. Abolition of Slavery.—Sec. 1. *" Neither slavery nor involuntary servitude, except as a punishment for crime whereof the party shall have been duly convicted, shall exist within the United States or any place subject to their jurisdiction.*
Sec. 2. *" Congress shall have power to enforce this article by appropriate legislation."* (Adopted in 1865.)

ARTICLE XIV. Right of Citizenship.—Sec. 1. *" All persons born or naturalized in the United States, and subject to the jurisdiction thereof, are citizens of the United States and of the State wherein they reside. No State shall make or enforce any law which shall abridge the privileges or immunities of citizens of the United States;*

nor shall any State deprive any person of life, liberty, or property, without due process of law, nor deny to any person within its jurisdiction the equal protection of the laws.

SEC. 2. " *Representatives shall be apportioned among the several States according to their respective numbers, counting the whole number of persons in each State, excluding Indians not taxed. But when the right to vote at any election for the choice of Electors for President and Vice-President of the United States, Representatives in Congress, the executive and judicial officers of a State, or the members of the Legislature thereof, is denied to any of the male inhabitants of such State, being twenty-one years of age, and citizens of the United States, or in any way abridged, except for participation in rebellion or other crime, the basis of representation therein shall be reduced in the proportion which the number of such male citizens shall bear to the whole number of male citizens, twenty-one years of age, in such State.*

SEC. 3. " *No person shall be a Senator or Representative in Congress, or Elector of President and Vice-President, or hold any office, civil or military, under the United States, or under any State, who, having previously taken an oath as a member of Congress, or as an officer of the United States, or as a member of any State Legislature, or as an executive or judicial officer of any State, to support the Constitution of the United States, shall have engaged in insurrection or rebellion against the same, or given aid or comfort to the enemies thereof. But Congress may, by a vote of two-thirds of each house, remove such disability.*

SEC. 4. " *The validity of the public debt of the United States, authorized by law, including debts incurred for payment of pensions, and bounties for services in suppressing insurrection or rebellion, shall not be questioned. But neither the United States nor any State shall assume or pay any debt or obligation incurred in aid of insurrection or rebellion against the United States, or any claim for the loss or emancipation of any slave, but all such debts, obligations, and claims shall be held illegal and void.*

SEC. 5. " *Congress shall have power to enforce, by appropriate legislation, the provisions of this article.*" (*Adopted in* 1868.)

ARTICLE XV. RIGHT OF SUFFRAGE.—SEC. 1. " *The right of citizens of the United States to vote shall not be denied or abridged by the United States, or by any State, on account of race, colour, or previous condition of servitude.*

SEC. 2. " *Congress shall have power to enforce this article by appropriate legislation.*" (*Adopted in* 1870.)

ADDITIONAL AMENDMENTS

The following amendments have been added to the Constitution since the last edition of Hart's little book was published. We leave the reader and teacher to study these amendments in the same way that the previous ones were examined.

Amendment 16 - Status of Income Tax Clarified. 2/3/1913

The Congress shall have power to lay and collect taxes on incomes, from whatever source derived, without apportionment among the several States, and without regard to any census or enumeration.

Amendment 17 - Senators Elected by Popular Vote. Ratified 4/8/1913.

The Senate of the United States shall be composed of two Senators from each State, elected by the people thereof, for six years; and each Senator shall have one vote. The electors in each State shall have the qualifications requisite for electors of the most numerous branch of the State legislatures.

When vacancies happen in the representation of any State in the Senate, the executive authority of such State shall issue writs of election to fill such vacancies: Provided, That the legislature of any State may empower the executive thereof to make temporary appointments until the people fill the vacancies by election as the legislature may direct.

102 AMENDMENTS TO THE CONSTITUTION

This amendment shall not be so construed as to affect the election or term of any Senator chosen before it becomes valid as part of the Constitution.

Amendment 18 - Liquor Abolished. Ratified 1/16/1919. Repealed by Amendment 21, 12/5/1933.

1. After one year from the ratification of this article the manufacture, sale, or transportation of intoxicating liquors within, the importation thereof into, or the exportation thereof from the United States and all territory subject to the jurisdiction thereof for beverage purposes is hereby prohibited.

2. The Congress and the several States shall have concurrent power to enforce this article by appropriate legislation.

3. This article shall be inoperative unless it shall have been ratified as an amendment to the Constitution by the legislatures of the several States, as provided in the Constitution, within seven years from the date of the submission hereof to the States by the Congress.

Amendment 19 - Women's Suffrage. Ratified 8/18/1920.

The right of citizens of the United States to vote shall not be denied or abridged by the United States or by any State on account of sex.

Congress shall have power to enforce this article by appropriate legislation.

Amendment 20 - Presidential, Congressional Terms. Ratified 1/23/1933.

1. The terms of the President and Vice President shall end at noon on the 20th day of January, and the terms of Senators and Representatives at noon on the 3d day of January, of the years in which such terms would have ended if this article had not been ratified; and the terms of their successors shall then begin.

2. The Congress shall assemble at least once in every year, and such meeting shall begin at noon on the 3d day of January, unless they shall by law appoint a different day.

3. If, at the time fixed for the beginning of the term of the President, the President elect shall have died, the Vice President elect shall become President. If a President shall not have been chosen before the time fixed for the beginning of his term, or if the President elect shall have failed to qualify, then the Vice President elect shall act as President until a President shall have qualified; and the Congress may by law provide for the case wherein neither a President elect nor a Vice President elect shall have qualified, declaring who shall then act as President, or the manner in which one who is to act shall be selected, and such person shall act accordingly until a President or Vice President shall have qualified.

4. The Congress may by law provide for the case of the death of any of the persons from whom the House of Representatives may choose a President whenever the right of choice shall have devolved upon them, and for the case of the death of any of the persons from whom the Senate may choose a Vice President whenever the right of choice shall have devolved upon them.

5. Sections 1 and 2 shall take effect on the 15th day of October following the ratification of this article.

6. This article shall be inoperative unless it shall have been ratified as an amendment to the Constitution by the

legislatures of three-fourths of the several States within seven years from the date of its submission.

Amendment 21 - Amendment 18 Repealed. Ratified 12/5/1933.

1. The eighteenth article of amendment to the Constitution of the United States is hereby repealed.

2. The transportation or importation into any State, Territory, or possession of the United States for delivery or use therein of intoxicating liquors, in violation of the laws thereof, is hereby prohibited.

3. The article shall be inoperative unless it shall have been ratified as an amendment to the Constitution by conventions in the several States, as provided in the Constitution, within seven years from the date of the submission hereof to the States by the Congress.

Amendment 22 - Presidential Term Limits. Ratified 2/27/1951.

1. No person shall be elected to the office of the President more than twice, and no person who has held the office of President, or acted as President, for more than two years of a term to which some other person was elected President shall be elected to the office of the President more than once. But this Article shall not apply to any person holding the office of President, when this Article was proposed by the Congress, and shall not prevent any person who may be holding the office of President, or acting as President, during the term within which this Article becomes operative from holding the office of President or acting as President during the remainder of such term.

2. This article shall be inoperative unless it shall have been ratified as an amendment to the Constitution by the legislatures of three-fourths of the several States within seven years from the date of its submission to the States by the Congress.

Amendment 23 - Presidential Vote for District of Columbia. Ratified 3/29/1961.

1. The District constituting the seat of Government of the United States shall appoint in such manner as the Congress may direct: A number of electors of President and Vice President equal to the whole number of Senators and Representatives in Congress to which the District would be entitled if it were a State, but in no event more than the least populous State; they shall be in addition to those appointed by the States, but they shall be considered, for the purposes of the election of President and Vice President, to be electors appointed by a State; and they shall meet in the District and perform such duties as provided by the twelfth article of amendment.

2. The Congress shall have power to enforce this article by appropriate legislation.

Amendment 24 - Poll Tax Barred. Ratified 1/23/1964.

1. The right of citizens of the United States to vote in any primary or other election for President or Vice President, for electors for President or Vice President, or for Senator or Representative in Congress, shall not be denied or abridged by the United States or any State by reason of failure to pay any poll tax or other tax.

2. The Congress shall have power to enforce this article by appropriate legislation.

Amendment 25 - Presidential Disability and Succession. Ratified 2/10/1967.

1. In case of the removal of the President from office or of his death or resignation, the Vice President shall become President.

2. Whenever there is a vacancy in the office of the Vice President, the President shall nominate a Vice President who shall take office upon confirmation by a majority vote of both Houses of Congress.

3. Whenever the President transmits to the President pro tempore of the Senate and the Speaker of the House of Representatives his written declaration that he is unable to discharge the powers and duties of his office, and until he transmits to them a written declaration to the contrary, such powers and duties shall be discharged by the Vice President as Acting President.

4. Whenever the Vice President and a majority of either the principal officers of the executive departments or of such other body as Congress may by law provide, transmit to the President pro tempore of the Senate and the Speaker of the House of Representatives their written declaration that the President is unable to discharge the powers and duties of his office, the Vice President shall immediately assume the powers and duties of the office as Acting President.

Thereafter, when the President transmits to the President pro tempore of the Senate and the Speaker of the House of Representatives his written declaration that no inability exists, he shall resume the powers and duties of his office unless the Vice President and a majority of either the principal officers of the executive department or of such other body as Congress may by law provide, transmit within four days to the President pro tempore of the Senate and the Speaker of the House of Representatives their written declaration that the President is unable to discharge the powers and duties of his office. Thereupon Congress shall decide the issue, assembling within forty eight hours for that purpose if not in session. If the Congress, within twenty one days after receipt of the latter written declaration, or, if Congress is not in session, within twenty one days after Congress is required to assemble, determines by two thirds vote of both Houses that the President is unable to discharge the powers and duties of his office, the Vice President shall continue to discharge the same as Acting President; otherwise, the President shall resume the powers and duties of his office.

Amendment 26 - Voting Age Set to 18 Years. Ratified 7/1/1971.

1. The right of citizens of the United States, who are eighteen years of age or older, to vote shall not be denied or abridged by the United States or by any State on account of age.

2. The Congress shall have power to enforce this article by appropriate legislation.

Amendment 27 - Limiting Congressional Pay Increases. Ratified 5/7/1992.

No law, varying the compensation for the services of the Senators and Representatives, shall take effect, until an election of Representatives shall have intervened.

OTHER SOLID GROUND TITLES

We recently celebrated our eighth anniversary of uncovering buried treasure to the glory of God. During these eight years we have produced over 250 volumes. A sample is listed below:

Biblical & Theological Studies: *Addresses on the 100th Anniversary of Princeton Theological Seminary in 1912* by Allis, Machen, Wilson, Vos, Warfield and more.
Power of the Pulpit by Gardiner Spring
Princeton Sermons by Aiken, Green, Hodge, Patton, Warfield
Thoughts on Preaching by James W. Alexander
Notes on Galatians by J. Gresham Machen
The Origin of Paul's Religion by J. Gresham Machen
A Scientific Investigation of the Old Testament by R.D. Wilson
Theology on Fire: *Sermons from Joseph A. Alexander*
Evangelical Truth: *Sermons for the Family* by Archibald Alexander
A Shepherd's Heart: *Pastoral Sermons of James W. Alexander*
Grace & Glory: *Sermons from Princeton Chapel* by Geerhardus Vos
The Lord of Glory by Benjamin B. Warfield
The Person & Work of the Holy Spirit by Benjamin B. Warfield
The Power of God unto Salvation by Benjamin B. Warfield
Calvin Memorial Addresses by Warfield, Johnson, Orr, Webb...
The Five Points of Calvinism by Robert Lewis Dabney
Annals of the American Presbyterian Pulpit by W.B. Sprague
The Word & Prayer: *Classic Devotions from the Pen of John Calvin*
The Christian Warfare by John Downame
A Body of Divinity: *Sum and Substance of Christian Doctrine* by Ussher
The Complete Works of Thomas Manton (in 22 volumes)
A Puritan New Testament Commentary by John Trapp
Exposition of the Epistle to the Hebrews by William Gouge
Exposition of the Epistle of Jude by William Jenkyn
Lectures on the Book of Esther by Thomas M'Crie
Lectures on the Book of Acts by John Dick

To order any of our titles please contact us in one of three ways:

Call us at **205-443-0311**
Email us at **sgcb@charterinternet.com**
Visit our website at **www.solid-ground-books.com**

www.ingramcontent.com/pod-product-compliance
Lightning Source LLC
Chambersburg PA
CBHW050537280326
41933CB00011B/1622